Reading: CHAOS AND CURE

Reading:

chaos and cure

Sibyl Terman / Charles Child Walcutt

McGraw-Hill Book Company, Inc.

NEW YORK / LONDON / TORONTO

To the Phoenicians,
who are said to have invented
the alphabet

Preface

Every fall millions of five- and six-year-olds go to school with sharp pencils and bright eyes—eager to learn to read. Three months later they are bored, frustrated, and either listless or disorderly, for they still have not started reading. Instead, they are being subjected to unnecessary exercises in hearing, noticing, and "experiencing" which are presumed to ready them for reading but which in fact only tire, confuse, and disappoint. Three years later the majority of them still cannot read.

The newspapers teem with reports of the nations's belief that the schools have failed in the fundamentals—and so have failed to prepare our ablest youth for the intellectual and scientific careers that now appear not just a luxury, or a right of democracy, but a condition of survival. We agree wholly with these fears and these charges. Indeed we believe the situation is much worse than even the alarmed citizen thinks it is. Every social gathering of educated parents reveals problems of adjustment, worries, and a growing sense of family responsibility to teach the children what the schools have not taught and yet what they say the parents should not try to teach. Juvenile delinquency is on the rise, and the disorder in the classrooms has increased to where competent teachers confess doubts of their ability to command attention.

We are, however, troubled by the solutions currently suggested: more money for school buildings, more money for teachers, more money for college scholarships, and the new drive to throw out the delinquents and the youth who are "filling our schools without learning anything." The first three are laudable, the fourth, as we shall explain, very alarming; but none of them gets to the root of the problem, which is *reading*.

With a system that has never been successful, our public schools have retarded the reading of the average child at least two years—and probably more—behind what it was forty years ago (when, let it be firmly stated, every child went through the first eight grades as surely as he does today), to say nothing of sending forth from our grammar and high schools millions of young people who cannot read well enough to cope with an average novel or the New York *Times*. Because they have not taught reading the educationists have by way of compensation altered the curriculum and indeed the whole concept of education to maintain schools in which, year by year, less use has been made of reading. It has come to the point where a young man can graduate from many of our major high schools, with superior grades, who not only cannot read successfully but also has not been called upon to do substantial reading in any subject.

Meanwhile the educational specialists rationalize. They now affirm that about one-third of our youth—and, they emphasize, often youth of superior intelligence—are congenitally unable to master the printed word. They have elaborated a program of "Life Adjustment" which begins with the assumption that, because more than half of our youth will not enter professions where learning and prosperity go hand-in-hand, these destined unfortunates should not be given the sort of liberal education that will make them unhappy with their modest lives. Public-school administrators have gone so far as to assert that they look hopefully for the day when learning to read will not be considered more

important than learning to sew or skate. Even the word
teaching has been expunged from some college catalogues
—and in its place appear "Guided Learning 1," "Guided
Learning 11," and so on—the explanation being that children cannot be stopped from learning and that the teacher
must simply guide the eager young along the paths they
democratically choose for themselves. These are far from being the worst absurdities that we have come upon in educationist literature.

If we are to draw a very grim picture, therefore, in explaining the present status of reading in our schools, we
shall, in later chapters, describe successful systems that
have years of tested results to demonstrate their effective-
ness; we shall tell what can be done to hasten the inevitable
change in our schools; we shall present a phonics system
with which the worried parent can teach his own five- or
six-year-old, or reclaim his "problem reader" from further
frustrations; and especially we shall try to equip the interested parent (and citizen) with a full and clear understanding of the current system of reading instruction and why
it does not succeed. In brief, this is intended to be a very
practical book, full of concrete evidence and specific remedies.

It is absurdly easy to teach a child to read with the proper
method. Most of the children in America could be taught in
a few weeks or months at the age of five. We shall tell you
about various schools, now functioning, where a problem
reader is virtually unheard of. . . . How, then, could our
schools have got into their present distress? A few undi-
gested concepts from Gestalt psychology, a pocketful of
ready abstractions (reading is a "developmental task"), plus
the belief that in a democracy everybody is entitled to everything from citizenship to culture—these have converted our
schools into playgrounds of experiment run wild. As for reading, the specialists had to make a big deal, a production, a
scientific program, and a "complexfunctionalaspect" of growth

and adjustment out of what should be merely the *training of a simple skill*. The skill got lost in the shuffle. They have libraries, bibliographies, clinics, electrical gadgets, guidance services, psychologists, psychiatrists, and neurologists—and these mountains of human and physical paraphernalia merely shut out the light and keep them from seeing the simple elements involved in teaching a simple skill.

We shall have to wade through a good deal of nonsense in trying to penetrate this chaos; but we hope the journey will have its amusing vistas and a rewarding end.

Sibyl Terman
Charles Child Walcutt

Contents

Reading: CHAOS AND CURE

One / The Reading Controversy

THE PROBLEM TODAY

The reading problem concerns more Americans today than anything but the H-bomb and major-league baseball. Millions of parents are worried; controversial literature on the subject appears every month; and the last word has certainly not been said. Rudolf Flesch has spoken in *Why Johnny Can't Read*, published in 1955, for which he continues to be attacked upon a wide variety of counts. Scores of articles have assailed him, and more recently a whole book has appeared whose authors admit that Flesch is their main target and inspiration.

We say the last word has not been said because we believe that the whole matter is still profoundly obscured to both laymen and educators. The average parent who is concerned about his child's reading has, for example, been told by the local school that he must not interfere at home with the work that is being carried out in the school. When he has brought up the delicate point of the criticism of current teaching methods, he has been told that the critics are not experts and that they do not have the qualifications to speak on a subtle and complex problem to which a multitude of experts have devoted "years of scientific research." And when he presses his questions he is answered in language that he cannot understand and with explanations that he cannot test.

We believe that reading is not taught properly today, and that the results of current methods are usually poor and often disastrous. We have written this short volume to set forth in the simplest language at our command the answers to the questions that are being asked. Our purposes are:

1. To show why the established theories of reading instruction, which guide most of our public schools, are in error and how the practices based on these theories have brought about the present deterioration of reading.
2. To explain how the schools should teach reading and to show what results can be achieved if sounder methods are employed—methods that are not *merely* a return to the "horse and buggy" practices (successful as they were) of fifty years ago.
3. To show in some detail how you can teach your own child to read, painlessly; how you can prevent him from becoming a retarded reader (as an almost unbelievable number of the young are today); and what to do if your child's reading is already a problem.

We do not at any point in this volume criticize the dedicated teachers who devote their lives to our children. If our comments on the theorists and experts who are immediately responsible for the formidable deterioration of reading seem severe, and if our tone is sometimes harsh, it is because we are impelled for the sake of the children whose abilities are being stifled to bring our findings to the American people. Far from criticizing the nation's teachers, we speak particularly to them, for they have been trained to use methods that subject them to frustration in their work and continual trouble with parents. They should be released from these exasperations—and they can be.

We should like to emphasize the fact that our message is full of hope and cheer, for there is mounting today in the United States a real tidal wave of reform and improvement.

We have investigated schools in several states where a number of new reading systems are being used with results that traditional educationists claim are impossible. These systems, furthermore, are perfected, published, available, and far easier to use than those which are currently confusing children in the schools which stick to the established methods. Our own system has been used for teaching reading and remedial reading for twenty years. The facts, in short, are available; if an enlightened public expresses its views on the problem, there will be a major reform within a very short time. It is already occurring, and its impetus will grow.

The most successful of the new systems and experiments are described at some length in Chapter 10. Chapters 11 and 12 show how reading can be well taught with relatively little effort, how the emotional barriers of a retarded reader may be leveled, and how the literacy of a family may be assured. The phonics system presented in the last chapter of this volume is simple, easy to use, and yet so comprehensive that it will teach a five-year-old or solve the reading problems of a college student. We present it here because we have found it the simplest and most effective of many that we have examined.

Our schools have made enormous progress in many areas. They now understand better than they did a generation ago how children learn and how they feel. The best of our modern teachers have done wonders in improving children's social adjustment. They have used discoveries about the psychology of learning, proper motivation, and fitting the learning task to the child's intellectual and emotional readiness. But these very real gains in method and understanding have generally been neutralized in connection with the teaching of reading because the theorists have not been able to recognize basic fallacies in their theories and practices. These practices are based, we believe, not on scientific research, but on their unwarranted extrapolations from research by psychologists.

For example, here are three assumptions (repeated everywhere in the literature on reading) which underlie current practices. They are that:

1. The average child of six does not *hear* sounds well enough to discriminate among them; so he must go through a period of ear training before he is ready to read;
2. The average child of six does not *see* well enough to discriminate objects as small as letters; so he must be tested and trained in this skill before he is ready to read;
3. The average child of six has not had enough experience to enable him to "bring meaning to the printed page," that is, to understand written material; so he must be taken on conducted tours of bakeries or farms to give him such experience.

These three fantasies, though only a sampling from among dozens, are basic, and we believe that they entitle the layman to question (and indeed to reject) the body of doctrine that rests upon them. It is often difficult to believe that the authors of some of the most imposing books on reading ever directly observed a child of six or reflected upon their own childhoods.

WHAT IS A SUCCESSFUL READER?

At a large private university which has an outstanding School of Education, we asked a professor who specializes in the teaching of reading the following question: "In an ideal first-grade teaching situation—small class, plenty of space, lots of equipment, and with no children of less than average intelligence—what would you consider a satisfactory proportion of your pupils *not* to be reading at all by the end of the first grade?" Her answer was 25 per cent. If that many had made no start in reading, she would consider it proper and satisfactory. This was under conditions that the professor herself defined as ideal and with pupils who would have an intelligence rating above the national average, and with *none below the norm* of an I.Q. of 100. (This means that they would rank in the upper half of children their age in the nation!)

These same children would by the end of the second year be reading in primers with controlled vocabularies of 500 or 600 words, although it is certain that a considerable number (possibly half) would know fewer than 300 words. The children who had learned no reading by the end of the first year would be lucky to know 200 words by the end of the second grade; the others would range up from 200 words, with a very few bright or advanced ones reading on a fourth-grade level in books with controlled vocabularies of up to about 2,000 words. At the same time, in most public schools today it is possible to find children in the fourth and fifth grades still working in primers and first readers. This group—and we have seen more than one school where it includes 25 per cent of the class—has still really made no progress in reading; they are forgetting words as fast as they are learning them, and unless there is a radical change in their instruction they will continue to be seriously retarded and end by ceasing to make use of any but the simplest reading in their lives.

The thinking behind these results was demonstrated to us in an interview with a "demonstration teacher" in a model first grade. We asked the same question: "In an ideal demonstration class, at the end of the first grade, how many would you be satisfied to see not reading anything?" The answer was that if 25 per cent were reading only in their own project books she would be satisfied. These books are made by the child as part of the "reading readiness" program. He pastes pictures in them, and the teacher writes some captions and perhaps a few sentences from the child's dictation. What he "reads" from his own project is a few words he has dictated; he reads them from memory, of course, and if they are all he can read it is certain that he would not recognize them in another book. These same children could not read in preprimers. Now we asked this teacher what she thought about a school nearby, in which the teacher told us that by March of the first grade the lowest pupil in her class tested at 2.0 (i.e., beginning second grade) and the best at 4.5 (middle of fourth grade); many of these children moreover were only five years old. The upper 75 per cent were reading freely in library books.

Her answer was, "Well, what *else* are they doing in the first grade? Were they having group experiences?"

We replied that they were happy children, obviously enjoying their reading. Then we described the results in one Eastern private school in 1945, where at the end of the first grade the children tested from 2.0 to 4.7.

"Oh, but that is a group of children from privileged homes," she said. "Those children have had a great deal more experience to draw upon in their reading."

Our definition of a successful child reader contrasts dramatically with these modest expectations. A successful child reader, assuming average intelligence, is one who can recognize in print, quickly and effortlessly, all the words in his speaking and listening vocabulary. This is not 400 but from 6,000 to 10,000 words, and this ability can be achieved during the first grade for many and the second and third grades for the rest. If he is a bright child, he will have tremendously increased his vocabulary from his reading; but if he is just average he will still be able to read all the words he knows.[1]

---

[1] Estimates of typical children's vocabularies differ so widely that we have offered what we consider conservative numbers here, although they have seemed too high to many readers of our manuscript. A leading authority, Dr. Robert H. Seashore, gives the following figures (a "basic" word would be *know*, with *knowing, knew*, etc., "derived"):

Grade	Basic	Derived	Total
1	16,900	7,100	24,000
2	22,000	12,000	34,000
3	26,000	18,000	44,000
12	46,500	33,500	80,000

(From "How Many Words Do Children Know?" *The Packet*, II, November, 1957.)

A recent book on reading, R. M. Goldenson, *Helping Your Child to Read Better*, Thomas Y. Crowell Company, New York, 1957, says that a typical

He will, furthermore, be able to read [2] paragraphs of material that he does not understand either because the vocabulary is too advanced or the ideas too complex. While the child in the demonstration school has been baking cakes and running a model farm, or visiting the local factory or garage so that he will have accumulated the experience which we are told he has to have before he can want to read or know what he is reading about, the child who is just taught to read via alphabet, syllables, and words will be able to read thousands of words and will be assimilating all sorts of experiences out of his books at a tremendous pace. Thus at an accelerating speed will his experience outstrip that of the child in the reading-readiness program. Nor will this unfortunate child *ever catch up* with the child of equal intelligence who has been reading for years on his own. The schools say that these slow starters are reading better in the sixth grade, because they have been taught to read for meaning. Actually they are still learning phonic clues for sounding out new words, and on the average they will continue to lose ground to the "successful" readers we have described, who are already so far ahead as to be out of sight.[3]

Interviews with many teachers convince us that in the New York City schools today half the children finish the first grade able to read only a few words. This is a generous estimate. If it were not possible for the child to learn faster, it would be proper not to bother him at all with reading so early—and indeed the theory of reading readiness points toward just this solution. But when the child could not only

---

child, aged seven, at the end of first grade, "uses about four thousand different words in her speech," can instantly recognize about a thousand words (in print), and can "actually grasp almost ten times that number through the use of word attack skills." This is obviously not the typical child we have observed. These figures illustrate the range of estimates current.

[2] In the sense, of course, of pronounce—a standard use of the word.

[3] A friend just back from England had his boy in kindergarten in what we should call a public school. At the end of the year he tested 3.9 on the standard American reading test; thus his reading equals that of the *average* American child at the end of third grade. This boy loved his school but was not outstanding in his class!

be reading all the words he knows by the time he is seven
or eight but also be learning hundreds of new words through
his reading, the waste of human potential is distressing. Nor,
as we have said, is this waste confined to the first year. Children in a great many schools—probably the majority in the
nation—are struggling with the beginnings of phonics in
the third grade. The writers have been told by a recognized
authority that it is "soon enough" if our school children are
learning to sound out words by the third grade. Thus years
of great potential are allowed to slip by when the average
child, curious, eager, and alert, could be expanding his awareness and enriching his life if he were only taught to read
properly.

The testimony of one of our wisest ladies, Pearl S. Buck,
may not be out of place here. Speaking of her youngest daugh-
ter, she says, "she has rejected a fair amount of the education offered her, as most American children do, and until she
reached high school I did not know whether to be exasperated
with her or with the teachers. Why, oh, why can learning
not be made more exciting, more rewarding? I was exasperated with her teachers when she came trudging home
from school, weary and pale with too many hours out of the
sunshine, and yet with a pile of books under her arm. What
wickedness, I cried in my heart, to keep a child sitting on a
hard bench all day and then crowd the night hours, too, with
homework! The children of Europe sit through long hours,
too, but they have more to show for it than our children
have. They achieve a prodigious amount of book learning,
they can speak several languages, they understand mathematics and the abstractions of philosophy, but our poor children end their school days with pitifully little in the way of
sound knowledge. I rebel against the waste of time . . ."

And here she comes to her considered thoughts on reading, in a passage of the greatest significance:

And I cannot remember at all when I learned to read. I know
I read quite comfortably at four, because on my fifth birthday I

received a small book as a gift, entitled *Little Susie's Seven Birthdays* and I envied Susie for having seven instead of five. Yet my American children learned reading with strange difficulty, and I am shocked at the number of our people, men and women, but especially men, who read slowly, word by word, and are never comfortable in reading and do not enjoy it, although the purpose of education should be to make reading as simple and easy as listening to a voice, for only when a person can really read will he surely continue his own education. And examining into the cause for this slow and painful reading I am convinced that it is chiefly because we have wasted the value of the alphabet. Today's children—or perhaps it is yesterday's, since my own, except for the one whom we call our little Postscript, are past the early grades—are taught reading as though each word were a separate entity, exactly as Chinese children are taught their ideographs, or characters, of which five thousand must be separately learned before one can read, and for this reason the Chinese need two more years than we do with our alphabet language. . . . But English is a matchless language, and the alphabet, each letter with its own sounds, is the key, yet in this generation the teachers have thrown the key away. I rebel, I say, though very little good does the rebellion of the lay mind do against the professional . . .

When our Postscript came along, a little German war child, I taught her secretly at home how to read, but I knew better than to mention it abroad. Her teacher . . . told me the other day that our child, though only in second grade, is reading fifth grade books and needs no help whatever. I smiled and kept my counsel. Of course she knows how to read, and knowing she enjoys it. She learned as I learned, easily and unconsciously, for I gave her the key to reading, as my mother gave it to me, by teaching her how to use the alphabet.[4]

THE CERTIFIED SPECIALIST

Close to our hearts in writing this book is the goal of furnishing the average interested layman with information and

[4] Pearl S. Buck, *My Several Worlds: A Personal Record,* The John Day Company, Inc., New York, 1954, pp. 355–357.

arguments that will enable him to cope with the jargon of the educationists [5] when they explain their methods. By cope we do not mean refute, exactly. We shall be pleased if our readers emerge feeling that they understand the problem.

Recently we heard a Board of Education Reading Consultant speak to a New York parent group. The speaker explained that modern methods were based on years of the most painstaking research by scientific specialists. She told the audience that teachers of reading today were "certified, just as doctors and lawyers are." Reading, she said, is a growth process, a complex and intricate activity, part of a highly integrated language-arts program which regards it as a functional tool answering the needs of developing children. The program is constantly studied by "consultants," who refine its perfections. After more of this dazzling but meaningless exposition, there was a question period. The parents asked, "What about the alphabet?" "Pooh," said the consultant, "I never learned the alphabet." "How do you use a dictionary?" she was asked. "Why," said she, "a child learns that experimentally, when he is doing research in the fifth

[5] We use the word "educationists" to indicate the professors of education who develop and expound the theories which flourish in modern schools and departments of education in our colleges and universities. These are the theories that control our public schools. The people in question do not like to be called educationists; they call themselves educators. But all teachers are educators, although the term has generally been used to designate professors in higher education. The dictionary defines an educationist as one versed in theories and methods of teaching; the word has had this meaning since the early nineteenth century, and there is nothing disgraceful or insulting in it. The word "educator" is a much more general classification which should not be narrowed to indicate, specifically, members of departments of education because to do so would leave no word to designate the professors of history, English, chemistry, and mathematics who are properly designated by it.... There is another motive for our choice: the educationists have, by calling themselves educators, quietly assumed authority over educational theory, matters of curriculum in the public schools, and indeed the whole question of how our young should be taught. Truer perspectives can be restored if we reserve the term "educator" for all the faculties of higher learning—and emphasize by the term educationist the specialization of our theorists.

grade; if he can't find a word immediately, he will look at several other words on the way to it, and this adds to his vocabulary. Furthermore," she continued, "I'll bet that if I name various letters, none of you people can tell me what letters come before and after them in the alphabet." The group indignantly insisted that they most certainly could do just that. "Well," she said, "what letter is missing on a dial telephone?" "Q, of course." "Oh, you heard a quiz program."

Someone then asked about phonics, and the consultant answered with references to the ear-training activities of the "reading-readiness" program! Next she spoke of certain "quacks," writing in the slick magazines, who wanted us to go back to the horse and buggy days of reading. Apparently she referred to the articles by Dorothy Thompson that appeared in July, October, and November, 1956, in *The Ladies' Home Journal*, which we found brilliant and enlightening.

The consultant next patiently explained that good readers saw words as wholes, indeed saw four or five of them at a glance—which was why the experts recommended that children be taught whole words initially. Here the confusions between the *learning* process and the *reading* process, between initial perception and later recognition of words, between seeing and understanding, multiply to the point where the average parent is baffled; but if he will bear with us we shall try to straighten out all these concepts in simple language.

SOME POLITICAL IMPLICATIONS

Here we might also speak of the brute question of survival. We are falling behind Russia in the training of scientists to an alarming extent. It is true that we have been far ahead for a long time and that we have a back-log of talent upon which to draw; but already the industrial demand for young scientists is outrunning the supply, and in the crisis the availability of accomplished science teachers and professors is bound to decrease just when the flood of rising college enrollments makes it more necessary than ever that we be able to teach them well. There can be no question that many young people who have the ability to become successful scientists never make the attempt because they have not learned to read well enough to cope with science texts and scientific prose. Automation will not solve this problem; we must have young people who can read well enough to become specialists.

Americans are generally openhanded. We like to spend our own earnings, and we do not object to large-scale spending by the government when we see that it is contributing to the nation's comfort, health, and culture. Our educational system, because of wars, depressions, and the rising birth rate, has not maintained its capacity to provide for our youth. Everywhere in the country we see classes increasing in size, teachers overworked and therefore less productive, schools operating on divided sessions in order to teach two schools in one building, and a spreading stain of worry, anger, and frustration. Federal aid to education has been delayed for a variety of reasons; and precisely because it may come in the near future, we must think today about how the money will be spent. The truth is that our present "underprivileged" public educational system wastes an appalling amount of money. Millions go into schools, buildings, equipment, and services—and what comes out does not justify the expense. It is true that we are not spending enough on education, particularly on salaries; but figures have been assembled that show that we spend something near fourteen times as much per student on equipment and nine times as much per student on teacher salaries as we spent seventy-five years ago. This increase has not been justified by educational gains, for the average child in an average fourth or fifth grade today does not read as well as he would have forty or sixty years ago. If we pursued this waste into remedial teaching, rooms for remedial reading in our schools, salaries for remedial teachers, plus the fact that thousands of young people are slowed down to the point where they cease to make any but the most limited practical use of reading, we should come to a staggering waste of dollars.

And the waste proliferates. It becomes a habit. When children have not been started correctly, so that large proportions of them cannot read well enough to learn, the understandable reaction in our schools is to *wait*—to give them something else to do until they catch on. We do not want sports, music, art, crafts, dancing, educational movies, and even some trips taken out of the curriculum. The point is that an hour a day spent on reading in the lower grades can be made productive of much better results than we are now getting.

It is possible for a student of slightly above-average intelligence today to graduate from high school with above-average grades, even though his reading is not adequate for adult reading. This can be true only if educational levels are prodigally debased. Before the nation contributes further millions through Federal aid, we should be sure that the money will not go to strengthening the system that is so unproductive now.

Two / How Bad Is the Reading Problem?

Nearly every piece of educationist literature says that reading has never been taught so well, that children today read far better than they did a generation or two generations ago, that children today read many times more books than they used to, and that continuing scientific experiments under rigidly controlled conditions are justifying and improving current methods. In short, again and again we read that *there is no reading problem;* the matter is in competent hands; the public should stop worrying.

One statement we have read and heard frequently and confidently from apologists for today's reading instruction is that current methods were introduced precisely because reading was taught so poorly forty years ago, producing a race of drudging little word-callers who gasped out words letter-by-letter and got no idea of the meaning of what they tried to read. Today, we are repeatedly told, reading is better taught and better learned. Now, we have incontrovertible evidence that reading skills have declined over the past forty years, and we should like to establish this startling fact before we go any further. For it must be remembered that the average primary school teacher today has from two to three more years of college training than she had forty years ago, and that our schools today have something like ten times

14

as many dollars' worth of plant and equipment per student as they had then. Furthermore, the school population today does not differ; substantially everybody went to school through eighth grade forty years ago, just as he does today. Do not be misled by the statement that many children forty years ago left school after the eighth grade; we are dealing with the way reading is taught from the first through the sixth grade:

The first edition of the Stanford-Binet Intelligence Test appeared in 1916, the second edition, revised, in 1937. One part of this test asked the child to read a paragraph within 35 seconds and recall eight facts in it with no more than two mistakes. This subtest was placed at the ten-year level, the criterion being that 60 per cent of ten-year-olds could "pass" it. Today a third edition of the Stanford-Binet test is being prepared by Dr. Maude Merrill James, who coauthored the second edition and did most of the work on it. Retesting present-day California children, she finds that whereas the other tests bring the same results, this reading test now has to be put at the twelve year level. At the age of twelve, 60 per cent of California children can today perform on a test what 60 per cent of ten-year-olds could perform on the same test in 1916 and at the time of the first revision in 1937. It must be emphasized that these children score on all the other parts of the test at the same level that they scored in 1916 through 1937—so they are children of the same average intelligence—but *they have fallen two years behind in reading.*

We do not have evidence on other states yet, but we should be surprised indeed if they can demonstrate that they are outperforming a state with the fine schools and high salaries that California has. California, incidentally, is ardently pro-Progressive in its educational philosophy and practice.

While the children of California—and apparently the rest of the nation—have fallen behind to this extent, we are

tempted to present a bit of contrasting evidence. In the public schools of Franklin Square, Long Island, reading is taught
by one of the best phonic systems we know—a system that
is quite contrary to present orthodox methods. (It is described at some length below, page 139.) Here in the spring
of 1957, in a third grade of 645 pupils, 80 per cent scored
above the national norm for children of that grade, on the
standard reading test. Their average scores placed them
more than a year beyond average national reading performance; and equal numbers of children in first and second
grades showed the same superior performance. Of this same
group of third-graders, 79.5 per cent made I.Q. scores of 100
or above. (22 missed the I.Q. test; 128 scored below 100.)

It is, of course, possible to conclude that these are children of markedly superior intelligence who therefore make
superior reading scores. But the community seems to be a
very average community, and the principal of the schools
does not think the children are of distinctly superior intelligence. Can it be that they make these impressively high I.Q.
scores simply because they have been taught to read better
than the children in typical public schools? Although not
proved, this conclusion is tempting, particularly because it
supports and corroborates our conviction that good reading
is absolutely basic to every kind of academic and intellectual
growth. (These scores were made on the Kuhlman-Anderson
group test. We do not of course suggest that the I.Q.'s are
actually raised by superior reading, but that superior training made superior performance.)

Turning from this objective and, we believe, unshakable
evidence, let us go behind the scenes and read the textbooks,
written by acknowledged experts for teachers in training.
Listen to Paul Witty, Professor of Education at Northwestern
University, prolific scholar, leading expert for twenty years
in progressive methods of teaching reading:

A condition similar to the one so strikingly revealed among
these college students is found generally among high-school stu-

dents and in adult groups. For example, studies show a wide range in ability to read and a large amount of reading retardation in the modern high school. Thus, a study of 7,380 graduates from the eighth grade in one large city showed that 2,169 were reading at or below the sixth-grade level. Other studies of high-school pupils reveal that, in many high schools, fully one-third of the pupils read poorly, and about 15 per cent are seriously retarded. In 1951, the following condition was reported as typical for high-school Freshmen: ". . . Two per cent of the pupils score below fourth-grade norms, and 48 per cent below the eighth-grade norms or tests."

At the college level, too, many students need help in reading. Thus, Triggs found that, in a large state university, 20 per cent of college Freshmen read at or below the eighth-grade norms. Many other students, of course, read so slowly that they could obtain little satisfaction or enjoyment from reading. Their range of ability was very great; and there were many able students who needed further guidance and direction in reading.[1]

Another leading specialist, Arthur I. Gates, of Teachers College, Columbia, asks:

Why are defects and deficiencies in reading so numerous? Why should a subject so important and so much studied be so difficult to teach and learn? Why do we find so many pupils, some of superior intelligence in the very best schools and under exceptionally able teachers, failing to learn to read satisfactorily? [2]

Or William S. Gray, Professor of Education at the University of Chicago, author of the famous *Dick and Jane* series of reading texts, says:

Records of the achievement of pupils show that from 20 to 30 per cent of the pupils who enter either the junior or senior high school read so poorly that they can engage in required reading activities only with great difficulty. Indeed, some of them

[1] Paul A. Witty, "The Improvement of Reading Abilities," Chapter X of the 55th *Yearbook of The National Society for the Study of Education,* Chicago, 1956, pp. 252–253.

[2] Arthur I. Gates, *The Improvement of Reading,* The Macmillan Company, New York, 1949, third edition, p. 3.

are so much retarded in reading that it is impossible for them to read the books ordinarily used at their respective grade levels.[3]

We have talked to many teachers—young ones, experienced ones, and principals—who have begged for advice on how to do something for the gravely retarded readers in their classes. A sixth-grade teacher in a relatively privileged California community described seven children in his class of thirty who were still stumbling in their second readers. One high-school teacher said that in his school only the top 20 per cent could read the standard texts for their grade.

One of the authors served for five years on a committee made up of parents, teachers, and administrators, established to study and make recommendations for reorganizing the teaching of English in the local public schools. The teachers said, again and again, that the children could not read. They could not read *Ivanhoe*, which had been on the ninth-grade program for many years; and the teachers had to read it to their classes. *Macbeth* was taught in the eleventh grade; again, the complaint was that the students simply could not read it. One teacher said that only selected classes, composed of the ablest students, could read their eleventh-grade texts. These texts, furthermore, as we shall show, represent a reduced and humble estimate of what eleventh-grade students ought to be able to read, for they are planned to be easy enough for the eleventh grade of any community in the country. On this committee, business employers asked why the colleges had not taught students to read; the college professors asked why the high schools had not taught students to read; the high-school teachers upbraided the primary teachers.

The authors have found that almost any small social group of, say, three or four sets of college-educated parents will reveal one—and often more—children with such serious reading difficulties that the parents are consulting specialists,

[3] William S. Gray, "The Language Arts—Reading, " *Implications of Research from the Classroom Teacher,* Washington, 1939, p. 138.

employing remedial teachers, or just worrying while they wait for the sudden burst of improvement that the school, as like as not, has told them will come if they are patient.

At this point it must be stressed that reading retardation does not correlate closely with I.Q. In a great school system like that of New York City there will, of course, be many children reading badly or not at all because they are of very low intelligence. Of this we are well aware. But experienced remedial teachers are unanimous in their agreement that the children brought to them for help—and needing it badly— are nearly always of better than normal intelligence and frequently *very superior*. This means that bright children usually have bright parents, who see that something is wrong and usually try to do something about it. What about the lower half of the population?

When the Army launched the great draft at the beginning of World War II, it discovered that between ten million (over twenty-five years old) and sixteen million (over twenty years old) Americans were unable to read up to fourth-grade level! By 1943 a million draftees had been rejected for illiteracy and three-quarters of a million had been accepted who read at or below a fourth-grade level. These millions could not all have come from Al Capp's mythical communities in the Southern mountains.

Confronted by this evidence, leaders in the field of reading wrote a symposium of articles that were printed in the *Elementary English Review* (XXIX, April–June, 1942). Their answer is summarized in this paragraph by Professor Dolch:

To the question, "What should the schools do about the poor reading on the part of our young men, as shown by the tests given draftees?" the answer is very simple. The schools should keep on doing just what they are doing and do it more widely and energetically.[4]

[4] "What Shall We Do about Reading Today?" by E. A. Betts, E. W. Dolch, Arthur I. Gates, W. S. Gray, Ernest Horn, Lou La Brant, Holland Roberts, Dora V. Smith, Nila B. Smith, and Paul Witty, p. 225.

There has indeed been, here and there, increasing recognition among educationists of the seriousness of the condition reflected in these appalling figures. For example:

It is no professional secret that as many as 40 per cent of the pupils cannot read a textbook written for use at a given grade level.[5]

And ...

However, the unpalatable fact is that some 600,000 of the 2,-000,000 children who will start to school this fall will develop reading problems before they reach high school unless the teaching and learning of reading takes a sudden turn for the better.[6]

A high-school principal writes:

In one city the Director of Curriculum reported recently that, "On the basis of standardized tests given to all students from grade one through grade 12, we will have to say that 72 per cent of our pupils are inadequate readers." In a Western Pennsylvania college last year, 20 per cent of the Freshman Class were required to take remedial reading courses, *without credit,* so that in the judgment of school authorities they would be able to read well enough to complete successfully their college program. Think of that! In a college class where most of the students came from the upper 50 per cent of their high school classes, 20 per cent needed remedial reading.[7]

While we are speaking of averages, it is well to point out that the national "norm" of reading ability, by which the educationists designate a child's progress, is the statistical mid-point. Half the children are above it, half below it. It is no cause for pride if half the children in your town score above the national norm for their grades, nor for shame if half score below it. The significant question is *what quality*

[5] E. A. Betts, *Foundations of Reading Instruction,* American Book Company, New York, 1946, p. 568.

[6] Fay Adams, Lillian Gray, and Dora Reese, *Teaching Children to Read,* The Ronald Press Company, New York, 1949, p. 388.

[7] Glenn McCracken, "Have We Overemphasized the Readiness Factor?" *Elementary English,* XXIX (May, 1952), p. 271.

of reading does the national norm represent?—and we shall show in Chapter 10 how far it is below what it could be. We know of one state that has devised its own reading test, with easier standards, so that in many communities the average child scores a year above his grade.

A still more significant question is the relation of any child's intelligence to the reading progress he has made. There *is* cause for alarm when we read in *The New York Times* that 42 per cent of the pupils who entered New York's academic high schools in the fall of 1955 were reading below their potentials. The majority were one and one and a half years below their estimated potentials, and 6 per cent were three or more years behind. This is a more alarming statistic than the one reported in the same article—that 55 per cent of 47,000 New York pupils were reading below national grade norms, 36 per cent were more than a year below, and 12 per cent were more than three years below; for when a pupil is reading below his potential, something is deeply wrong.[8] Here are some specific cases from our files—including the sons of three successful elementary-school teachers:

Tommy A had attended a private school for five years (six, including kindergarten) when his mother taught there in the fourth grade. When Tommy had been in her own class through the year, she came to us because she was worried about his reading and had not been able to help him herself as she had hoped to do. On a Stanford-Binet Intelligence Test, he scored an I.Q. of 155, which is attained by about one child in 500. His mother was astonished at this score, because she had become convinced that Tommy was a "slow learner." He tested fifth grade on the "paragraph comprehension" part of the Stanford Achievement Test, yet when he was asked to read the same paragraphs aloud we found that he was completely unable to pronounce the long, important key words upon which the meaning depended. But he had written down the right answer every time! Reading

[8] *New York Times*, December 14, 1955, p. 45.

was a guessing game for Tommy, and with his intelligence
he had developed phenomenal skill at it. Early in the year,
we had offered to work with the boy and teach him some
phonics, but his mother said, "No, he has had so much of
phonics that he is sick of it." At the end of the school year,
we gave Tommy four hours of drill with our phonic system.
Then Tommy went off to a ranch where he did not look
at a book all summer. A week after school opened in the fall,
he again took a Stanford Achievement Test; he still tested
fifth-grade in reading, but on the geography, history, and
word-meaning tests he had gone up about four years since
spring. After the test he went home and said to his mother,
with a broad smile, "That's the first time I ever knew what
the words on that test meant." In January of that school year,
without any further special instruction in reading, Tommy
read Wells's *Outline of History*. Less than a year earlier (the
previous June) we had had to go back to a third-grade reader
to find a book that Tommy could read acceptably. Tommy's
mother admitted rather sheepishly that she now could see
that he was brighter than other children.

Henry B also went to a private school where his mother
taught fourth grade. When we saw him briefly at the age
of eleven, with an I.Q. of 162 (attained by one individual
in 8,000), he had to have help with two words in every
three in a fourth-grade reader. There were only two words
in the language, *the* and *to*, that he recognized instantly;
others he could say only after he had spelled them out aloud,
and not always then—this in a fourth-grade reader. When
Henry was fourteen, his mother told us that he had at last
learned to read; but investigation disclosed that he then
tested fifth-grade in reading and read very slowly and hesi-
tantly, guessing at many words that were in his speaking vocabulary. Unlike Tommy, he did not have remedial help.
High school and college were a struggle for him, although
he did finally graduate from Harvard at twenty-four. He

decided against graduate school because reading was so difficult.

Chester C is the son of a professor in one of the outstanding university education departments in this country. Chester read scarcely at all until he was ten. His mother did not ask for help, but she reported that he was one of those children who developed slowly, who achieved "reading readiness" later than the average child. In the fifth grade he was reading with pleasure books on the fourth-grade level, having made some rapid progress during the past year. These books were adventure stories, with interesting material and a carefully controlled vocabulary; with his I.Q. of 150 he could easily have been reading these books when he was six.

Alice D, a delightful, well-adjusted child—who loved school, who always shone in music, art, and handicrafts as well as leading her class in the academic subjects—was the pride and comfort of her teachers. She had learned to read early; she read fluently and extensively in all sorts of good books, including the best of children's literature. She is the sort of child to whom modern schools would point with pride as a proof that they really do turn out superior readers. She did not learn to read before she went to school; she was the perfect exhibit of the "system." On no grounds could she have been considered a reading problem. . . . Yet when she was given the Stanford Achievement Test in fifth grade and made a score of 7.0 (seventh grade), she finished in eight minutes instead of taking the twenty-five minutes allowed for the test. Every written response was absolutely correct: she didn't guess or skip; she answered all the questions on paragraph comprehension, correctly, up to the seventh-grade level. And there she stopped.

Knowing that her I.Q. was 145 (one in 250), and aware of her extensive reading, we had expected her to test higher; and so we asked her why she stopped where she did, after only eight minutes. She replied, referring to the succeeding paragraphs, "I don't know those words." Two hours of instruction and practice in attacking long words and pronouncing them would have enabled Alice to score tenth or eleventh grade on this test—where she should have been, according to her mental age. Tommy, it will be recalled, tested only two years below Alice, but he did so by working hard for twenty-five minutes and guessing furiously at every paragraph, using a high order of reasoning ability to make up for his ignorance of words.

We have known students in leading universities of this nation who have *paid* people to read to them, not because they were blind but because they could not recognize the words themselves. All, of course, had to be of superior intelligence to get into such institutions; they had made high marks in high school; and they were earning high marks in science and mathematics. Evidence of this sort could be piled up indefinitely to show that our schools are failing with a serious proportion of our *gifted* children.

In a private conversation, a high-school superintendent said: "The A lanes contain 20 per cent of the students; they are good and the teachers like to teach them. The R lanes contain 30 per cent of the students; they are hopeless. In between we have the B lanes, the middle 50 per cent. There is a wide range of ability among them. But on the whole they cannot read, they cannot spell, they cannot write a decent sentence. The teachers don't know what to do with them because they have already formed so many bad habits and are so discouraged, yet they all expect to go on to college." The real truth is, then, that not 20 per cent or 30 per cent, which William Gray quotes (page 17), but closer to 80 per cent of our high school students are more or less illiterate. And furthermore, in the words of an educational psychologist:

Now we know, after testing thousands of students, that a large portion of them are struggling along without the reading skills they need. Many more can read just well enough to keep up with the everyday demands of school, but few students in any grade are anywhere near top efficiency.[9]

Perhaps the most convincing—although by no means statistically reliable—evidence that reading has gone downhill of late years comes when we raise the question among a group of middle-aged reminiscers. Parents, teachers, college professors, superintendents, librarians agree emphatically that it has. There is evidence from every level and walk of life that we have a reading problem of tremendous importance.

[9] Lee J. Cronback, *Educational Psychology*, Harcourt, Brace and Company, Inc., New York, 1954, p. 143.

Three / A Variety of Explanations

We have shown in the last chapter that many people are dissatisfied with the present state of reading, and we have touched on the fact that there is a vast sunken reservoir of very poor readers who have pretty much eschewed the printed word and yet whose limited educations have taught them only to blame themselves for their intellectual shortcomings. What, now, of the various brands of specialists who might be supposed to speak with authority on the reading problem? What do they say is the matter?

Explanations of the shortcomings are as various as they are interesting. Doctors frequently accept the theories of Dr. S. T. Orton,[1] who spent thirty years working with children and adults who had difficulties with speech, reading, and writing. He established the term *strephosymbolia* (meaning "twisted symbols") to designate a condition in which a patient with normal intelligence and years of training, who was unable to read, displayed the key symptom of reversing words, syllables, and letters, both in reading and writing. A victim of *strephosymbolia* who would read and write *saw* for *was* or *ton* for *not*, or who could not read at all (afflicted with *alexia*, i.e., nonreading), had, according to Orton's

[1] S. T. Orton, *Reading, Writing, and Speech Problems in Children*, W. W. Norton & Company, Inc., New York, 1937.

hypothesis, inherited a tendency to fail to develop complete dominance of one cerebral hemisphere over the other.[2] Dr. Orton deduced his explanation from the fact that adult patients with brain injuries displayed the same symptoms as nonreaders. Dr. Roswell Gallagher, in *Understanding Your Son's Adolescence* (New York, 1951), includes a readable, nontechnical presentation of this theory, with several case studies of children to whom it presumably applies. The theory is badly shaken when such children are quickly taught to read by a phonic method.

Psychologists and doctors have devoted a good deal of study to the theory of "mixed hand-eye dominance" as a major source of nonreading. This condition, also termed "mixed lateral dominance," exists when a child is right-eyed and left-handed (or vice versa), or when a left-handed child has been retrained to write with his right hand, and sometimes with ambidextrous children because they are presumed not to have a single linked dominance by one side of the brain and one side of the body. Some students of the problem considered it a major cause of reading retardation and nonreading, but the best psychological opinion is that this condition in an extreme form occurs in a very small per cent of the population, whereas some degree of it obtains in the majority of the people. We have observed that occasionally a child who was strongly left-handed and left-eyed and was trained to write right-handed had difficulty with reading. But we have observed many retarded readers—indeed the majority of them—who do not have pronounced mixed hand-eye dominance; and psychologists have reported enough cases of the condition who learned to read easily and well to conclude that it is not a substantial explanation of the problem. Parents have largely ceased to force their left-handed children to change, but the reading problem lives on.

---

[2] Technically, alexia is a specific type of aphasia: a defect in the brain, either inherited or acquired by injury, that prevents reading although the person can hear and talk and even spell words.

Many psychiatrists believe that most children who fail to learn to read, in spite of attending good schools, do so because they suffer from a hidden conflict or maladjustment. Relieved by psychotherapy, these children learn to read. The observations of doctors and remedial teachers, however, are that their emotional difficulties do not exist when the children come to school but develop as they fail to learn to read.

Dr. Grace Fernald, a psychologist who studied the reading problem, developed a practical method for curing non-readers—by having them trace words again and again until they could reproduce them independently—and from this worked out a theory that some children were predominantly kinaesthetic. That is, they had to learn through their muscles what other children learn through their eyes and ears. Her practical system was successful with a great many children. (Her method has deteriorated in the hands of some of her disciples to the point where they see kinaesthesia behind every bush and would have half the schoolchildren in America busily tracing and keep them at it for years.)

The belief that individual differences extend to the very physical traits employed in reading has developed (apparently from Miss Fernald's presumed discovery of the kinaesthetic type) a mythology of classification which now enjoys the status of fact among the educationists: children are now auditory, visual, or kinaesthetic; and if they are not taught according to their particular capacities they become retarded. We have come to the point where such tendencies must, apparently, be considered by every teacher. Here is a typical explanation:

A teacher who stresses the auditory approach over the visual develops in the child a slow method of word attack, which will be of help to him on only one out of every three words in the adult English vocabulary. A teacher who stresses the visual over the auditory establishes a quick method of word attack (inasmuch as it usually divides the word into fewer units and is not retarded by vocalization or subvocalization), which is nevertheless limited in application. Even when a teacher gives ample consideration to both of these, he may automatically produce poorer results, perhaps reading problems and cases of nonreaders, among these children who profit most by the method of tracing a word and getting a sense of its wholeness through feeling.[3]

This classification of children seems to us quite baseless. In the most successful schools today all children are taught by the same method, as we have said. All children use eyes and ears when they read, hands when they write.

School administrators have a variety of opinions gathered from various sources. Many of them are leaning toward the concept of the *nonverbal* type of child, who has normal intelligence, good social adjustment, reasonable ability in mechanical and handicraft skills, and performs well in arithmetic, but just does not get along in activities requiring reading and writing. According to an astonishing article in *Harper's Magazine* by George H. Henry, a high-school principal in Dover, Delaware, the schools have tried every conceivable method and remedy on these children, but they simply cannot be taught to read properly:

This is no diatribe against the schools. No method and no brilliance of teaching can improve these youths enough to make any appreciable difference in their literacy. By testing any graduating class or any high school in the country, the skeptic can see for himself what is an old story to teachers: that a third of the high school cannot read on a fifth-grade level . . .

The pupils who compose this lower one-third are not to be confused with the mentally backward (a far smaller group comprising only about five per cent of a school or less). The great

---

[3] C. M. McCullough, Ruth Strang, and A. E. Traxler, *Problems in the Improvement of Reading*, McGraw-Hill Book Company, Inc., New York, 1946, pp. 103–104. It is true that some adults *memorize* by ear, some by eye, and some by copying a passage over and over, although it is thought that such differences are due to training rather than inheritance. Where the untested classification leads to the unsupportable generalizations on word-attack in this passage, we are witnessing a diagnosis that has probably *caused* more reading difficulties than it has corrected.

majority of them are normal, wholesome, even talented, responsible youth. They are, to put it simply, nonverbal ... [people]
who for the life of them cannot master the mechanics of pronouncing and writing words.[4]

Mr. Henry concludes that high-school education in
America has "virtually collapsed," not because they do not
teach reading but because it *cannot be taught* to one-third
of our youth! Good remedial-reading teachers do not recognize a nonverbal type. These children can be taught to read.
The belief that they cannot is perhaps our most startling
insight into the confusion and demoralization that exists
today in our schools.

Rudolf Flesch, of course, says they haven't been taught
phonics, but as we shall show in detail later, there is today
no general agreement among educationists on what phonics
is or how it should be taught. Even before Mr. Flesch's book
appeared, intelligent laymen were complaining that their
nonreading children could not sound out words properly, did
not use the alphabet effectively, and guessed at meanings
when they should have been pronouncing words.

The educationists run through a gamut of explanations,
depending on their audience and the kind of reading disability under discussion. Publicly they insist that their methods
are excellent but that crowded schools, bookless homes, un-
cultured or neurotic parents, poorly trained teachers, stupid
children, juvenile delinquents, and the presence in their
schools of a great mass of children who used to drop out
and go to work after six or eight years of schooling account
for the failure of these methods to produce a uniformly high
level of reading success. ... Their one fundamental explanation, repeated everywhere in their writings, is that the child
who failed to learn did not have "reading readiness" when
he started; beyond this, however, they reiterate that "the
causes of reading disability are many, subtle, and complex,"

[4] "Can Your Child Really Read?" *Harper's*, CXCII (January, 1946), pp.
72, 75.

and they proceed to enumerate causes in lists like the following:

1. Physical Defects
2. Emotional Factors
3. Lack of Interest
4. Meager Experiental [sic] Background
5. Lack of Reading Experience [5]

or in more ambitious lists like this:

1. Mass Teaching
2. Organic Defects
3. Organic Conditions Which Are not Really Defects
4. Deficient Psychological Processes.
5. Constitutional Immaturity
6. Lack of "Reading Readiness"
7. Unfortunate Forms of Motivation
8. Failure to Acquire Essential Techniques
9. Ineffectual Types of Teaching
10. Unfortunate "Accidents" in the Process of Learning.[6]

whose author explains that

A good reading examination today would include a careful case history, certain tests and opinions given by other specialists, and a number of tests developed during the past forty years by investigators of reading. An appraisal of vision and hearing by an expert in these fields and an overall medical examination would be routine. Occasionally an examination by a neurologist, psychiatrist, or clinical psychologist would be secured ... [and so on] ... One such diagnostic examination includes about fifty tests and examinations, most of them carefully standardized.[7]

These lists and procedures conceal by confusion the fact that these children just do not learn by present methods. When a friend gives you six reasons why he missed an ap-

[5] Glenn Meyers Blair, *Diagnostic and Remedial Teaching in Secondary Schools*, The Macmillan Company, New York, 1946, pp. 4–5.

[6] Gates, *The Improvement of Reading*, p. 4.

[7] *A Review of Rudolf Flesch, Why Johnny Can't Read,* The Macmillan Company, New York, 1955, p. 15.

pointment, you know that he has not given the real one. The
educationists' explanations of reading disability—of which
these are only random samples—are likewise so various as to
suggest a strenuous effort to control a flood that is breaking
through the dikes in all direction. They are defensive, apolo-
getic, and resentful by turns, and they strike out in every
direction—not even excepting the constant refrain that "we
do teach phonics!" and "reading is being taught better now
than ever before!" Set these beside the fact that teachers
often sum up the nonreader with the comprehensive "he
must have some terrible block"—and we see that the answer
is still to seek.

The extent to which the thinking of reading specialists
has invaded and influenced medical opinion on the subject
is demonstrated by the following passage from a current
authoritative textbook on pediatrics, widely used by medical
students:

READING DISABILITY

Reading disability is frequent, occurring in perhaps 10 per
cent of school children. It is usually manifested by any of the
following: mirror reading (reversed letter orientation), misplace-
ment of letters, word substitutions, sound-letter misassociation,
or faulty idea integration.

Etiologic Factors: Include psychogenic disturbances, ocular
defects, pathologic brain conditions, endocrine disorders, and
defective training. (Children should not be taught to read until
ready developmentally. Reading-readiness tests may be used to
indicate whether a child is ready to learn to read. This is usually
at about six and one-half years but may be one year earlier or
later.)

Treatment: A complete evaluation, including study of the
emotional status, an ophthalmologic survey, and psychometric,
neurologic, and audiometric examinations, determines the types
of treatment necessary.

All physical defects and psychogenic factors should be corrected. Special educational assistance should be given along with

the indicated psychotherapy. The education therapist must work hand in hand with pediatrician and psychotherapist.[8]

This is the entire passage on reading disability in this 500-page text. It reflects the basic educationist assumptions, and although it does include the phrase "defective training," it does not seem to give any importance to the idea, for disability is represented as physical and emotional. If your doctor has studied this standard text he may not be easy to convince that most reading troubles stem from teaching procedures.

In many books on the teaching of reading you will find it suggested that the eyes of the average child of six are not fully developed. For example one authority writes, "Focusing the eyes on the printed page is a complex task demanding both a degree of visual maturity which may not be achieved at the age of six and specific skill in coordinating the functioning of the two eyes." [9] Several educationists have assured us that this is due to the fact that myelinization of the optic nerve is not complete until the average child is six and a half years old. The myelin sheath is a white substance over a nerve that appears at different times on different nerves. Yet in Dr. F. H. Adler's *The Physiology of the Eye*, page 528, we read, "... although myelinization of the optic nerve fibers begins at about this time (fifth month

[8] Lawrence B. Slobody, *Survey of Clinical Pediatrics*, McGraw-Hill Book Company, Inc., New York, 1955, pp. 61–62.

[9] Margaret G. McKim, *Guiding Growth in Reading*, The Macmillan Company, New York, 1955, pp. 40–41. And see E. A. Betts, *Foundations of Reading Instruction*, American Book Company, New York, 1946, for an extended discussion of the problem . . . If one searches a bit, one can find anything on almost any side of any problem scientifically proved; for example, some studies of visual acuity and reading disability have discovered no close relationship. One investigator found that a group of good readers had poorer vision than a group of poor readers, another that a group of fast readers had the same vision as a group of slow readers. See H. M. Robinson, *Why Pupils Fail in Reading*, University of Chicago Press, Chicago, 1946, pp. 13–15.

of fetal life), it is generally not until the seventh month that this has progressed down the nerve as far as the lamina cribrosa." [10] Can someone have read "six months of fetal life" as "six years"?

Another passage in the same book perhaps comes nearer to the problem:

There can be little doubt that inability to obtain 20–20 vision in most children and in many clinic patients is due partly to their lack of cooperation and intelligence: in other words, it is due to a low power of attention. The accurate fixation needed to read the smaller letters on the usual office charts is likewise not developed in very young children. The letters on each line of the usual Snellen Test chart are printed in such a way that as they get smaller more are crowded on each line. The result is that in order to read the 20–20 line, accurate fixation of each letter is necessary in order to separate it from its neighbor. Children under six or seven generally do not have the necessary coordination of the ocular muscles to do this. [11]

This seems to make a case—until we consider what size type this would be that would test 20-20 vision and baffle the ocular muscles of a six-year-old child. Here is what it looks like:

A successful child reader, assuming average intelligence, is one who can recognize in print, quickly and effortlessly, all the words in his speaking and listening vocabulary. If he is a bright child, he will have tremendously increased his vocabulary from his reading; but if he is just average he will still be able to read all the words he knows. He will, furthermore, be

This might well prove too small for a child, but who ever saw a primer printed in this size type? Primer type is four or five times as large:

A successful child reader, assuming average intelligence, is one who can recognize in print, quick-

[10] F. H. Adler, *Physiology of the Eye*, C. V. Mosby Company, St. Louis, 1953, second edition, pp. 528–529.

[11] Adler, p. 625.

There is no scientific evidence that an average child of six would have the least difficulty seeing these letters and telling them apart. An average child of three could do so, easily.

According to specialized authority, 52 per cent of children between six and seven have 20-20 vision; they can read the *very small type* reproduced above. Between five and six, 38 per cent of children have 20-20 vision.[12] A practicing oculist corroborates these statistics, as well as the general conclusion that the average vision of a child under six years old is 20-30. This means that the average child *under* six can distinguish the letters of this type:

A successful child reader, assuming average intelligence, is one who can recognize in print, quickly and effortlessly, all the words in his speaking and listening vocabulary. If he is a bright child, he will have tremendously increased his vocabulary from his reading; but if he is just

—which is still considerably smaller than a child is asked to read. Children's Book Type requires only 20-60 vision, which is very weak vision indeed.

It should not be necessary to introduce all this scientific evidence to prove what any alert person knows from firsthand observation, but the specialists have claimed scientific authority for their contentions. We believe that the whole confusion stems from the fact that, as the authority quoted above says, children may not pay attention. When they have been taught their letters, they have no trouble seeing them. In practice, the mythical "fact" that the *average* child does not have adequate visual acuity for reading until he is six and a half is invoked to justify deferring the beginning of reading instruction until *all* children are six and a half, whereas at the same time it is used to *justify* the fact that half or more of the children in a school have made no beginning in reading until they were more than seven years old!

[12] *Vision of Preschool Children*, Publication No. 66 by the National Society for the Prevention of Blindness (1929), p. 18.

Four / How Reading Is Taught

So there is a reading problem of major proportions; and the experts' explanations prove that the experts do not know what the trouble is. It is now time to present our analysis and explanation. There *is* one single cause, and it is fairly simple to understand. Compared to the elaborate diagnoses we have quoted, it is simple indeed. Except in a small fraction of cases, it is not a matter of intelligence, of physiological defects, or of psychological disturbances. It is purely a question of *teaching method*. Almost all the reading disabilities we have described could have been prevented, and virtually every nonreader could have learned to read early, if he had been taught by the right method—or if he had *not* been taught by the wrong method.[1]

Let us therefore describe in detail how children are taught today, both in theory and in practice.

[1] The following definitions will be of help in understanding some of the terms used in this book:

Syllable: a single uttered sound made up of a vowel or a vowel-consonant combination and uttered with one breath impulse. A syllable like *arsh* contains three phonemes.

Phonogram: a representation by letters of a single speech sound, a syllable, or a word. We generally use the word to indicate a syllable.

Phonetics: the science of speech sounds.

Phonics: a branch of phonetics; it is the system of representing word sounds with letters.

Actually there are two somewhat divergent types of practice among modern educators. The extreme "progressive"
point of view and method are described in Margaret McKim,
Guiding Growth in Reading. The first-grade teacher begins
in the fall with a group of six-year-old children, whom she has
been taught to see as a group of individuals, each with his
own personality and problems, on widely separated levels of
maturity. She starts with a program which at first includes
no reading activities whatsoever but is devoted to a *project*
centered probably around some aspect of family living or
community activities. The children engage in play with cardboard, sand pile, drawing, painting, or simple carpentry,
through which each child is skillfully led to make contributions to the central project. There is a democratic atmosphere
in which the children help to plan their own projects and the
teacher acts as a leader, not as a top-sergeant type of disciplinarian. It is natural for a six-year-old to talk, to move
about, and to express his ideas through overt activity; that
is, when a child of this age gets an idea he immediately wants
to *do* something to express it in tangible form. The child is
therefore encouraged to express these impulses—in sharpest
contrast to the old-time schoolroom where the children sat
for hours in chairs screwed to the floor and where even
whispering was forbidden.

Once a day the children have a "sharing and evaluation
period" in which they express in words what they have done,
criticize each other's work, suggest improvements, and plan
the next steps. At the end of six weeks of this sort of thing,
under a really skillful teacher, the assorted mob with which
she started has been magically transformed into a happy social group. The show-off, the withdrawn child, the compulsive
talker, the timid, nervous child, and the baby who cried
when his mother left him on the first day have apparently disappeared and been replaced by a group of relaxed and happy
citizens, each of whom feels that he is part of the group, has
contributions to make to it, has learned to keep quiet and

listen when others are talking, and is not afraid to express
his own ideas before the group. There seems to be no occasion for discipline or punishment; and indeed the teacher
treats these children as courteously as she would her own
friends. A visiting parent has the reaction: "This is *right*
for six-year-olds."

Throughout the first year, group activities are organized
around projects which are considered meaningful for the
children. The teacher has been trained to size up each child
and decide which ones are ready to begin reading and which
ones must be given further "reading-readiness" activities—
some even through the whole of the first year—until they
have been brought to the point where they are "ready" to
begin reading. The social adjustment, the emotional adjustment, and the ability to listen and to present ideas verbally
are the first and fundamental steps in this "reading-readiness"
program. Other steps are getting the children to grasp the
ideas that printed words represent objects (equipment in
the school room has been labeled with signs reading *table,
chair, hammer,* and so on) and to know that their spoken
sentences can be written down in black and white. When
stories are read to the children, they perceive that print can
be converted into speech. They learn jingles which train them
to listen to sounds, to hear rhymes, and to discriminate words.
A good deal of time is devoted to making the children realize
that sentences are read from left to right.

In the extreme progressive program, the teacher prepares
the children's reading materials directly from the activities
through which they have been fused into a social group. She
encourages them to dictate descriptions of their projects and
experiences, which by skillful suggestion and selection she
converts into sentences of appropriate vocabulary and simplicity, such as, "We went to the bakery." "The baker made
a cake." "We ate the cake." "We liked the cake." Thus every
bit of reading is meaningfully related to the child's experiences. When such sentences are put together, beautifully

printed by the teacher on a big sheet of cardboard, to make
an account of a project, a game, or a field trip, we have what
is called an "experience chart." A typical first grade produces
quite a number of these experience charts and posts them,
decorated with the children's drawings, about the classroom.
The language, as we have said, has been carefully winnowed
by the teacher so that the vocabulary is as limited as possible
and as nearly as possible like the vocabulary of the basic
readers, although numerous big words are included; the sentences come out short and declarative, beginning as far as
possible with the same subject, as above. The experience
charts produced during the first year will present a considerable vocabulary.

The child is not supposed to learn to "read" these charts
in the adult sense of the word read, yet he is supposed to
know what they say. The teacher reads them to the class,
waving her hand from left to right always, under the sentences. Presently she calls a bright little girl or two up front
and asks, "Can you show me where it says, 'We ate the
cake'?" The child is carefully trained at this time to "frame"
the sentence with her hands instead of pointing, for if she
just pointed she might put her finger on *the* and the other
children might think that it meant "We ate the cake." It will
soon dawn on some bright or observant child (who has more
"reading readiness" than the others) that a certain configuration which means *cake* recurs at the end of three sentences.
We say "configuration" because no attention has been given
to the alphabet yet, and the child knows nothing of spelling
or letters. She observes the similarity of total shape, and she
deduces the fact that the word *cake* is always represented by
the same shape. She probably does not know this configuration well enough yet to recognize it in another context. Indeed, she is not expected to recognize it elsewhere—a point
which is carefully stated in the manuals.

In the course of subsequent months this collection of
experience charts is gradually *analyzed* into its parts. First

sentences have been "framed" and thereby identified. Then
the words in the sentences are located and identified as entities. Remember that the child's eyes, in the first grade, are
supposedly not capable of distinguishing or identifying letters; but as the process of analysis continues, they begin to
note the differences between strikingly dissimilar letters like
m and *t;* although the letters are still not given their names
because the emphasis must be kept upon meaning and the
whole. When the educated adult reads, he does not think
of the names of the letters in each word; indeed he sees the
word as a whole, instantly, a meaningful whole that is part
of a thought. This is what the child is being trained to do,
from the beginning. The process of learning to read is defined,
by proponents of this method, as "the ability to make finer
and finer discriminations"—and this is precisely what has
been taking place in the program that we have described.

Because meaning rests in words rather than in letters,
the ensuing months of reading instruction are devoted to
reading and rereading material containing a carefully selected and controlled vocabulary of elementary words. As
he reads these words again and again in various contexts, in
his primers and readers, the child becomes increasingly
familiar with them as individual entities or pictures, and he
gains speed in reading them. When the teacher is showing
the child how to tell one word from another, she uses "clues"
which are carefully described in the manuals—clues which
call attention to the shape of the word as an entity. To make
this perfectly clear, let us quote an authority:

First of all there is a series of visual clues, that is, helps in the
recognition of a word which may be secured by visual observation of the word. The typical clues usually mentioned are as follows:
  a. The total shape or configuration of the word. Thus, "on"
     and "or" are similar, but "on" is very different from "by"
     and from "automobile." There are characteristics of the word
     as a whole which are not to be found in the parts of the
     word alone, just as there are expressions characteristic of a

    person's face which cannot be located if one merely sees in turn the nose, the eyes, the mouth.

  b. Striking visual features, such as a tall beginning part, or a flat ending part; e.g., *th* in "this"; *oo* in "foot."

  c. The critically distinguishing features of very similar words, as in the case of "house" and "horse," "war" and "was," "sit" and "sat."

  d. The common visual elements in words which represent different sounds, as in the case of "war" and "ware," "fold" and "look," "now" and "row." [2]

This author goes on to describe phonic clues and the "structural analysis" of words into syllables for identification, but the emphasis continues to be on the recognition of the whole word as a visual and meaningful unit.

By this method, the overwhelming preponderance of time and effort is devoted to learning words as configurations. Proof of this statement is to be found in the fact that the process of analysis which is ultimately to equip the child to sound out a word purely through its letters *continues through a period of six years*—but even so the other clues come first. In this program the brighter child may know 1,000 words, as sight words, in the third grade, but he is by that time making only the *beginning* of "attacking" new words through the use of phonic (i.e., letter) and other clues. The readers which are being used during these years include lists of the new words with the pages upon which they appear. These words are "introduced" to the class—written on the board, pronounced, and defined—by the teacher before they are read in the book; a special term like *flintlock* or *muzzle-loader* is explained in detail, when the project is Daniel Boone, before it is read in a sentence among familiar words:

Here is how a teacher might introduce the word "boat" to her class. She would use a similar procedure with the other 50 to 100 words.

  [2] Arthur I. Gates, *A Review of Rudolf Flesch, Why Johnny Can't Read,* The Macmillan Company, New York, 1955, pp. 4–5.

The first step is to give the children some experience with the word at the oral level. Through a discussion of their various experiences with boats the teacher determines the extent of their understanding of the word. She may ask, "Who has seen a boat?" "When?" "What does a boat look like?" "What do we use boats for?"

The second step is for her to present the word orally and in printed form at the same time. A picture may accompany this presentation to insure understanding. The teacher will focus the children's attention on the word as she pronounces it. She may call attention to the initial consonant sound of *b* in *boy, book,* and so on.[3]

This induction into reading involves a formidable amount of drill, although the word is not used.

With its concern for the child as an individual and its great theoretical stress upon "individual differences," this system, of course, expects a wide range of performance among a typical group of children. In the sixth grade there will be children performing at levels from first to tenth grade. In the fourth grade children will be reading at levels from first to perhaps eighth grade, and so on. This spread is regarded as a *fact of nature,* a proof of "individual difference," indeed a proof of good teaching rather than otherwise. Everywhere in the literature the fact of individual differences is stressed. When children in the third and fourth grades, for example, are still in their primers, the fact stands as clear proof of learning differences. In any class from the end of the first grade through the sixth (in the extreme progressive school) you will find each child reading a different book, which is supposed to be adapted to his interests and ability. In the more conservative type of school, the children are divided into three reading groups, according to the level of their accomplishment, in which they read together from the same basic reader. Nowhere do you find the system that prevailed

[3] Sam Duker and Thomas P. Nally, *The Truth about Your Child's Reading,* Crown Publishers, Inc., New York, 1956, p. 89.

thirty years ago, where the entire class had a reading period during which the teacher called on one child after another at random to read aloud from the text which every other child held in his hands and followed. (The great sin was not to know the "place" when you were called on.) Some children do not have "reading readiness" until they are eight or even ten, and it would be a mistake to push them beyond their "developmental stage." There is great fear of *pushing* a child beyond his level, although the teacher is expected to work constantly with the child whose readiness has not flowered during the first year or two of schooling.

After six years of this program, average children will have reading vocabularies of approximately 4,000 words. *In theory* they have by this time, through the year-by-year, systematic introduction of word analysis and phonic attack, been equipped to identify and pronounce any new word they come upon. For what they can actually do the reader is asked to look again at the evidence set forth in Chapter 2. The brightest children will sometimes be reading magnificently; a few will be nonreaders; often they will be retarded. The less intelligent children will also show a considerable spread of reading ability, but on the whole they will be reading only simple prose material fluently. The great majority of sixth-graders who have passed through this program will find many common words that they cannot pronounce or understand.

We have said (page 37) that there were two "somewhat divergent types of practice among modern educators" on the teaching of reading. The second approach stresses readiness, reading for meaning, experience, and starting with whole thoughts (as sentences or paragraphs) which are analyzed down into words and ultimately letters; but it differs from the extreme progressive method in using a formal series of basic readers with workbooks full of exercises designed to teach the children what the progressive teacher undertakes to elicit from their group experiences. Less stress is placed on projects leading to experience charts. Whereas in the extreme progressive method reading may grow quite unconsciously out of a social-studies project on Daniel Boone (Eskimos are now out of style) or the dairy industry, often from material the teacher writes herself, the second method has formal reading periods during which the children work with their basic readers and do exercises in their workbooks. The second method puts the child through a prepared and predetermined course, but its method and theory are substantially the same.

A few words now about the psychological theories underlying this program: the basic emphasis on individual differences has been noted. Second, Gestalt psychology is supposed to demonstrate that the child learns *from wholes to parts;* that he can first discriminate an object or a person as a whole; later he learns to see parts in the whole—wheels in his toy car, fenders, and windows—by which he tells one whole from another. As he gets older he is able to make finer and finer discriminations, to tell which toy auto has a spoke missing and to distinguish between a 1947 Dodge and a 1948 Dodge. Here is how the latest spokesmen for the educationists describe the process:

We are teaching the child to respond to many kinds of differences in what he sees. The training leads to a general ability to respond to differences. What we are attempting to establish in reading is the habit of looking for and reacting to small visual differences. Soon the child will need to distinguish between *Bob* and *Betty,* between *ball* and *bell* and so on. It is important that he react to the significance of these differences because the sense of words is often changed by these *a*'s and *e*'s. "Ringing a ball" makes about as much sense as "bouncing a bell." But a child cannot be expected to make such fine visual discriminations until after he has developed the habit of making larger visual discriminations. . . . Reading, as you can see, is essentially a matter of making such visual discriminations and, as in the case of the toy train, two things are essential. First, the child must reach the level of maturity necessary to enable him to make the required discriminations; and, second, he must be provided with many opportunities to make them.[4]

This description represents the theory accepted by the leading experts for the past two decades. Applied to reading, the theory is that the child is presented with a *whole story* on an experience chart, which he is first led to recognize as the description of an experience that he dictated. Next he is led to pick certain sentences out of this whole; then individual words. He is led by the teacher, with consummate skill, infinite patience, and endless drill, to discriminate between *play* and *airplane*. The reading process is seen as a gradual development of the child's ability to "make finer and finer visual discriminations"—and also, as a corollary, to make auditory discriminations, such as that needed to tell *bell* from *ball*. This process of development, as we may judge from the quotation above, takes years, requires careful watching and management, cannot be left to chance, and is guided by methods that have evolved out of years of research and study by the leading experts. The reading-readiness program is specifically designed to bring the child's ability to make discriminations up to the level upon which he can begin reading and forge rapidly ahead to discriminate 300 words in a year.

According to this system, based on this psychology, it is *absolutely wrong and forbidden* to teach the letters first, because doing so would reverse the fundamental learning process. The child seeing letters instead of whole words (as the reading adult does) would have his attention captured by these small objects and fail to look at the whole words out of which meaning is made. This would be setting up absolutely the wrong habits and would get the child off, very seriously, on the wrong foot.

The firmness and assurance with which certain scientific findings on perception are invoked to guarantee the "scien-

---

[4] Duker and Nally, *The Truth about Your Child's Reading*, pp. 78–80. The critical fact is that children have made these steps when they are three.

tific" bases of current reading theory are clearly illustrated in the following paragraph—which contains the basic assumptions (and the basic errors) underlying this theory:

The way in which modern methods of teaching reading grew out of experimental investigations is a good illustration. Three discoveries made at different times between 1879 and 1910 are the fundamental, but not the only, bases upon which modern methods rest. One was the discovery that the eye, in reading, moves along the line by a series of starts and stops; the second, that the eye while at rest can take in briefly about an inch and a half of a line of print held at the ordinary reading distance; and the third, that one need not see distinctly all of the letters, or even all of the words, in an "eyeful" to recognize the group of words. These discoveries led to new methods in which were emphasized learning to recognize words as total configurations instead of letter by letter, learning to read by getting meaning directly from perception of the symbols without the intervention of oral reading or complete articulation of the words, and learning to utilize rapid and rhythmic eye-movement progressions along the line. Shifting from the old to the newer procedures has enabled both young and mature readers to improve the thoroughness of comprehension and to increase greatly the rate of reading.[5]

After a substantial number of words have been learned as wholes and the child has been drilled until he reads them rapidly and easily for meaning (though many continue to stumble over these first words), the training of discrimination will be taken on to letters and the other small visual clues for word recognition that we have presented earlier in this chapter. This ability to note the smaller clues is constantly aided by the teacher, who points out configuration clues such as "the two tall lines pointing up at the end of *ball,*" or "the curve at the beginning of *Sally.*" As one of the current texts says:

[5] Arthur I. Gates, Arthur T. Jersild, T. R. McConnell, and R. C. Challman, *Educational Psychology*, The Macmillan Company, New York, 1950, pp. 342–343.

Intelligent instruction will teach him to use effective techniques of word analysis so that he locates the most helpful letters and groups of letters in the form of the word, and thinks and uses the sounds of those elements in getting the pronunciation of the words. Such instruction will teach him always to use the context and word analysis in conjunction with one another, so that detailed analysis of a word as a rule is unnecessary, and so that he can check the result of his use of the context and the result of his use of word analysis against one another.[6]

We have dwelt upon this careful application of Gestalt psychology to reading because it is the very basis of modern theory and practice and, as we shall show, it comes from a misunderstanding and misapplication of the theory.

[6] The reader might consider how this procedure trains the eye-movements of a child.

Five / Why It Fails

As for my teaching experiences this year, I would say that they have been generally rewarding. And as to your pet subject—reading—I can now confirm that you are 101 per cent correct. Of the eight in my lowest group in third grade (all of whom possess over 100 I.Q.) the reason they cannot read is that they do not know the sounds. Yes, some are emotional problems, in fact they all are; however they do not know that a b is a b. But the problem basically is not that they do not know sounds, but rather that I am not allowed to teach them! My reading program is carefully supervised by a "specialist" who is comparable to the General in the Army. She commands—I obey or else. And since the teacher sits at the bottom of the pile (or should I say lies there worn, torn, and barely gasping) behind child, parent, administrator, custodian, specialists, etc., her thoughts (if she dares) must lie carefully concealed and masked lest anyone discover that she isn't a member of the smiling personality cult. But the job is financially rewarding and the kids are terrific. . . . We teachers are the most vulnerable people; so any change must come from the top.

(From an unsolicited letter from a former student.)

Normal children taught by these carefully worked-out methods, by dedicated teachers, ought to begin reading somewhere between the ages of six and a half and eight, and six years later should read simple prose fluently. Unfortunately, as we have shown, these modest goals are beyond a vast number of our twelve- and thirteen-year-olds, many of whom will be graduated from high school without achieving them.

We have described the educationists' explanation of this failure in Chapter 3. Their methods, they say, are excellent; the failures are due to the fact that for one reason or another these methods are not used, or the pupils are incapable of learning, or the home is at fault.

Let us look for a moment at the other side of the picture. There are schools where the less able children are ready, at the end of the first grade, for second readers and the best are reading widely on their own from children's books with unrestricted vocabularies. These are the Franklin Square, Long Island, schools where, last year, all but 43 of 558 first-graders were at or above the national norm and scores ranged up to 7.1. We have seen a child, entering first grade at five years and eight months, learn to read in six weeks so that she was voluntarily reading children's books of assorted vocabularies that were in her home. She was given training in phonics before any reading was begun. We visited her class, where there were more than thirty children, and discovered that she was not outstanding there. Furthermore, she taught her little brother and at four-and-a-half he was also reading easily.

A year and a half later this boy, then aged six, was entered in first grade at the demonstration school connected with a midwestern state normal college. The program for first grade there consisted of a full year of reading readiness, to which this boy was required to submit. The parents suggested that he be given special work or be put in second grade, but the teacher assured them that he "was no brighter than any other pupil in the class; he merely had *happened* to learn to read." *At the end of the third year,* his classmates, many just as bright as he, were still unable to sound out words that they had not learned as sight words and had reading vocabularies of well under a thousand words, whereas the strange boy could by then read anything he wanted to read.

One of the authors started various children reading with about the same pattern; two-thirds of the way through the primer they would take off and be reading on their own. We know of many other seven- and eight-year-olds who have taught their younger siblings in the same way. It has been with amazement that the authors have, during the past twenty years, learned of increasing numbers of equally bright children who are reading very badly (or not at all) after six years of progressive instruction by highly trained teachers in our public schools.

Any psychology of reading has to be able to explain these "phenomenal" children as well as the very bright and the normal children who have serious reading difficulties. Far from accounting for these "phenomenal" readers (they weren't even unusual thirty years ago and they still exist today) current theory scarcely acknowledges their existence.

Briefly and specifically, here is the heart of the matter: if you forbid the learning of letters and start with whole sentences and words, keeping the attention of the child on meaning, you will get certain reactions from your class; if on the other hand you start with a thorough grounding in the names, shapes, and sounds of the alphabet, and require the child to be able to print all of it before he starts reading, the whole picture will be different. All the official literature deals with the former of these programs. The experts have not really looked at a class of pupils learning by the latter method; they scarcely believe it can exist.

Teaching words as meaningful wholes ignores the very basic fact that *printed words are symbols of sounds* and are made of letters which are symbols of sounds. Current theory completely misses the fact that a printed word has meaning *because it is a symbol of a sound,* a spoken word, that already has meaning to the child. It is not the configuration that means; it is the sound, *which the child already knows.* He does not have to memorize the configuration of a word for

its meaning—as he is made laboriously and with infinite drill
to do today—he has to learn to recognize it instantly as a
sound. The instant he hears it, he knows it, and with the
alphabet as equipment he can learn to hear thousands of
words this way in a year or two at most, and *sometimes in a
few weeks.* By this process they become "sight" words, of
course, which the good reader sees instantly as wholes. The
modern experts have a mistaken notion of what it is they
are teaching the child when they teach him to read. They
undertake to teach him hundreds of picture-configurations
when it is incredibly faster, simpler, and more natural to
equip the child to *hear* the sounds he already knows when
they are symbolized on the printed page. This is how we
learned to read, so quickly that we hardly knew it was happening. This is how the thousands of people learned who
will tell you that they actually cannot remember learning
to read. This is how today's lucky children learn when they
learn in six months instead of six years.

Another way to grasp this analysis—which is the central
and most important point in this book—is presented in the
accompanying diagram. Three elements are involved in the
reading process; they are *objects* in the world, *spoken words,*
and *printed words.* The simple and logical way to read begins with the object and recognizes that a first grade child
has, by conservative count, already memorized 10,000 words.[1]
He has been working at this task all his waking hours for six
years, and he has learned all these words by ear. Each word
has been a new memory feat for the child, for the connection between, say, the object—chair—and the sound *chair* is
purely arbitrary: any other sound would do as well to designate a chair. But the second step—from the spoken word to
the printed word—is not arbitrary; it is logical and simple; it
consists of learning the alphabet, learning that letters are
sounds, and then getting the KEY of how letters are blended

[1] Estimates range from 10,000 to 24,000. The last figure seems *very*
high to us. See note 1, p. 6.

into sounds and words. By this route the child goes from the
sound that he knows and then *inductively* [2] proceeds through
letters and blends of letters to discover how the known sound
is represented in print. Of course he has to memorize some

[2] Induction and deduction both have their places in logic, science, and
education, for both are indispensable tools of thought. In reading instruction, the systematic build-up from letters to sounds to blends to syllables to
words can properly be called an inductive or synthetic approach, going from
parts to wholes; whereas the analysis of whole words, that have been learned
first *as wholes,* to identify and learn phonic elements in them, may properly
be called a deductive or analytical method. We use the terms in these specific
senses for this specific occasion only. Educationist writings do not agree on
whether the sight method is deductive or inductive, and we have no wish to
engage in that confusion.

THE RIGHT WAY

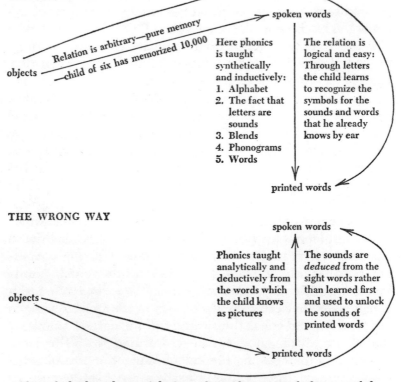

spoken words

Relation is arbitrary—pure memory
child of six has memorized 10,000

objects

| Here phonics is taught synthetically and inductively:
1. Alphabet
2. The fact that letters are sounds
3. Blends
4. Phonograms
5. Words | The relation is logical and easy: Through letters the child learns to recognize the symbols for the sounds and words that he already knows by ear |

printed words

THE WRONG WAY

spoken words

| Phonics taught analytically and deductively from the words which the child knows as pictures | The sounds are *deduced* from the sight words rather than learned first and used to unlock the sounds of printed words |

objects

printed words

This is the hard way because it begins reading with a new set of arbitrary symbols
(printed words) instead of using what the child already knows (spoken words)

equipment—the alphabet—but the symbolic representation of sounds by letters is a reasonable thing. As he masters the KEY, a first-grade child will very quickly recognize simple words *instantly* (*not* laboriously or with painful letter-by-letter groping, as the educationists say he will) when he sees them in print for the first time. A child who knows *hat* and *cat* and *bat*—and knows his letters—will not have to sound out *fat* when he first sees it printed; it will say itself to him almost automatically; it will fit into the meaning-hearing-saying pattern of his conditioned responses easily because he has already made the same adjustment, with the same letters, in learning scores of words. A pattern of response has been established, involving the child's whole knowing-communicating mechanism, which he easily extends to new situations of the same order. There is thus no mystery about why it is so easy to learn to read if one takes the proper steps.

Now let us look at the present "official" look-and-say approach, which the educationists now call the "traditional" method, in the light of these facts. Here the child is taken from the object to the printed word *directly* and begins learning a new set of completely arbitrary connections. He sees the word *green* as a color, not as a sound. The printed word *dog* does not resemble the animal; so the child is asked to begin all over again to repeat the feat of memory that accumulated his 10,000-word "ear" vocabulary. He is in literal fact beginning all over again. After he has learned these words-as-pictures—or call them words-as-meanings—for a year or two, his teacher begins to *analyze* them and *deduce* the phonic patterns from them. Now when a child knows the word *green* as a picture or shape, and knows what it means, there is no fun and no reward in laboriously going at it deductively to get at the sounds and the letters. Analyzing the little squiggles in words that he already knows by sight is a bore; he tires and loses interest. When the process is extended through three or four years, he is very likely to miss out on some parts of it. But worst of all, when his established

habits of word-recognition are disturbed (suppose, for example, he has memorized words by looking at the shapes of
the spaces *between* the letters—a method not in the least
unlikely when a child has begun learning words before letters) he may be confused and distressed to the point where
he refuses his attention. The transition from seeing a word as
a *total pattern* to seeing it as a *sequence of letters* may completely bewilder a child. At this point he is well on the way
to becoming a nonreader or a seriously retarded reader.

There are two thresholds where reading problems appear.
One comes during the first three years, when many children,
failing in the initial learning of sight words, are declared not
"ready" to read, with varying amounts of worry by their
parents and consequent emotional disturbances in the children. The second threshold comes when the child who has got
off to a satisfactory start in the first or second grade floun-
ders on the transition and reorganization of his habits involved in working on phonics deductively; that is, when he is
asked to see words as composed of sound-symbols (letters)
in sequence. It is marked by a slowing of progress that often
turns into regression and emotional distress. This second
threshold sometimes appears at the fourth or fifth grade
level, where the child who has been relying entirely on total-
word memory (presumably ignoring the "incidental" phonics
which his teachers have been dutifully slipping in from time
to time) finds that he cannot keep up with the accelerated
vocabulary growth in his graded readers. Others approach
this threshold having absorbed some phonic understanding
(we have interviewed many children whose use of phonics
consists of sounding the first letter of a word and guessing
the rest of it; others know a few common phonograms like
ite, ill, ed, and *ing,* but often only as they know sight words)
which breaks down under increasing demands made upon it
by more advanced reading. For these children, phonics is
merely a distraction or a frustration.

When you teach reading you start with a child who has

already learned to talk and has been communicating with
words for years. He has learned thousands of words which
are symbols for concrete objects, emotions, actions, relation-
ships, and qualities. The basic act of the reading process, the
fundamental skill, without which there can be no reading in
any sense whatever, is to be able to look at a printed word
and respond orally or silently with the corresponding spoken
word. What are the elements of this act, and how is the
skill acquired? The verbal response has already been learned
and *overlearned*. The child has learned to make discriminations between sounds with fantastic skill and great speed.
At six the average child hears more precisely (or pays closer
attention) than an adult—witness how he can repeat foreign
words that an adult misses. Ask your three-year-old whether
he wants a bell or a ball for Christmas, a goat or a boat, a
motorboat or an overcoat, an icicle or a tricycle, a blackboard
or a black Ford—and he will answer you instantly. Ask him,
"Do you want some ice cream, or should I scream?"—and he
will burst out laughing.

Now take the other part of the process, which is the
printed word—a visual image. The basic reading act is recognizing the visual image and forming a stimulus-response bond
between the visual image, the sound it symbolizes, and the
response already in his mind. This is the clearest possible
case of a conditioned response. The child sees *boat*, hears
boat, and says *boat* simultaneously. If the child knows the
letters already, the word is made of something he recognizes.
If the child knows that the letters are sounds, he knows automatically that the word on the page stands for a sound,
and thus reading is fitted into a pattern of speaking-hearing-
meaning with very little effort because the child has already
accomplished 95 per cent of the work in his years of growth
and learning.

For the child who does not know the alphabet either as
printed letters or as symbols of sounds, the word on the page
is a totally new squiggle that is presented to him as a *meaning*

and therefore as a completely new learning act that is not
related to anything else he knows—and particularly and
disastrously it is *not* related to his speech and hearing responses in a functional way upon which he can systematically
and naturally build. He makes responses at random, sees
boat and says *cow,* realizes that he has not satisfied his
teacher, and thus is thrown into confusion and discouragement. The kindly teacher cheers him up and goes into months
and years of training, leading him to see clues by which he
can learn these visual squiggles until he gets them straight.
The whole process seems to him extraordinarily arbitrary,
for he does not initially have any way of knowing *why* one
squiggle means *cow* and another *boat*. The vital link of
sound has been omitted. Why? Because sound is in the letters, and the experts' concept of Gestalt forbids beginning
with anything so small as a letter. It is a part, and they care
only for wholes.

But how can a child *possibly* learn that the printed word
red means the color red without automatically learning the
sound that connects the two? Particularly when any child
already knows the sound and has known it for years? It
would seem impossible. Yet this is just what many children
do. They miss the obvious precisely because it is so obvious.
Sounds are so universally involved in their lives that they
do not think about them. So there is not a simple *word-sound-
color* pattern established.

It is rather two pairs of patterns:

the printed word *red* ‹. . . . .› color red
and
color red ‹. . . . . .› sound red

Each of these pairings may be established in a child's mind
without the other connection of

the printed word *red* ‹. . . . .› sound red

being established. The child will relate the color to the
printed word; and he will from earliest childhood have made

the sound "red" when he saw the color; but he will not consciously connect the letters of the printed word with the
sounds in the spoken word until he has been taught. A child
learning to read by look-and-say may not (most do not) use
the knowledge of sounds with which he has lived all his
life. He will see the word *red* and think of the color without
realizing that the symbol stands for a sound—even while
he quite naturally and unconsciously indicates the color by
pronouncing the sound! This is something that has to be
thought about, but the mature reader can think of parallels
in his experience to bear it out.

The connection between the printed word and the sound
may not be realized until it is taught—and it apparently is
not so realized by more than half of our children in the first
two or three grades. The growth of this awareness in the
child may be somewhat parallel to the growth of language
itself. Some linguistic specialists have suggested that speech
began in chant and ritual without conscious meaning and
that meanings were attached to "words" later when their
part in a dance or ritual was stabilized and thereby related
to the meanings expressed in the dance. Children can learn
and use words without being aware of them as words. The
critical concept of words must be learned.

So complete is the experts' blindness to the fact that
printed words must first be considered and recognized as
symbols of sounds that a typical one says Rudolf Flesch
"offers little or no genuine evidence in support of his extravagant claims for his phonic panacea," adds that phonics
constitutes "a complex and synthetic procedure of building
up word parts," and concludes that phonics "slows the
reader" because "it tends to get children into the habit of
recognizing words piece-meal." [3]

Since a child can see letters and learn them as wholes
(millions of children have done so) just as he learns faces
as wholes, it is an arbitrary and unfounded warping of

[3] Arthur I. Gates, *A Review of Rudolf Flesch, Why Johnny Can't Read*,
pp. 15–17.

the Gestalt theory to insist that the wholeness and individuality of *letters* must be ignored. A child who has
a set of letter blocks can and will learn them, as wholes,
by playing with them. With a bit of encouragement he
can be led to reproduce them and to know the capital
and lower-case forms. With these wholes firmly in mind,
he is ready to approach words *synthetically,* which is the
way they are made: whether the experts like it or not,
writing in its formal or *mechanical* aspect is a synthetic
process of making words out of letters, and the child cannot
possibly become adjusted to this fact too soon.

Two further points must be made about the Gestalt theory
of learning:

1. Leading psychologists do not agree on the validity of Gestalt theory. Deductions from the theory are still more suspect.
2. The word-recognition method of reading is not a valid application of the Gestalt theory.

Evidence for these conclusions follows:

A psychologist who has conducted many experiments on
learning the International telegraphic code reports findings
that cast doubt on the validity of Gestalt theory. Significant
experiments were conducted with the size (and other aspects) of the learning unit. Some receivers were started on
letters in the code; others were started on whole words, from
which they might in time have been expected to deduce the
letter symbols. There were two findings: the learning of the
latter group did not proceed any faster, either initially or in
ultimate speed; and a considerable number of that group
could not learn at all. Here is a close resemblance to the
word-recognition procedure in reading. Since the goal of
telegraphy is to send and receive whole words, it would be
parallel to look-and-say theory to have the beginner start
by listening to whole words until he had mastered a number
of them and then encourage him to separate out the symbols
for letters. But it did not happen, and only the very "tal-

ented" learners could learn code at all by the method. Most
learners, the psychologist reports, either did not or could
not make any progress by the whole-word method. Another
experiment compared receiving nonsense words with receiving real words, as a training procedure. It was found that the
presence of meaning did not increase the speed of learning!
A beginner can be trained just as quickly, and to the same
ultimate speed of sending and receiving, whether he works
with real words or nonsense words. Mastery of the basic
skill is not affected by the presence of meaning.

Gestalt theory affirms that we learn by wholes because
our first perceptions, in any situation, are of wholes, in which
we proceed to make finer and finer discriminations of detail.
But Gestalt cannot arbitrarily specify the physical size of the
whole in any situation. Units of meaning in reading are
books, parts, chapters, pages, paragraphs, sentences, phrases,
words. There is no research to establish the size of the meaning unit that will "naturally" be apprehended first. Indeed,
the educationist literature does not distinguish between perception and learning in this matter.

Presented with a new configuration, we see the whole before we see the parts of which it is made. But we have to
learn letters before we can easily learn the words of which
they are parts. Here the Gestalt process may operate in time
rather than in space, and physical size may be incidental.
The temporal rather than the spatial relation determines the
learning process. The letter is *first in time* and therefore
(figuratively) largest even though it is spatially smallest.
Thus one must see the letters as wholes before he sees them
in larger patterns of symbolized sound.

One can "see" a Chinese face at a glance, but it is a com-
monplace that all Chinese look alike to a Westerner (just as
all Westerners look alike to a Chinese). In order to "see" a
Chinese face so that one can distinguish it and recognize it
on a later occasion, one must have learned its "letters"; that
is, one must know the characteristics that make for individ-

uality in Chinese rather than just the larger elements (yellow skin, slant eyes) which make them all look alike to us. One does not "learn" such a face as a whole. One learns it easily, however, if he is familiar with the sort of parts of which it is composed. Thus, seeing a Chinese face is not equivalent to knowing it; one could see a million Chinese faces without being able to distinguish them. But if one had learned the features (its "letters") first, one could tell Chinese apart quickly.

The educationists have nevertheless extrapolated from the Gestalt theory to designate the *paragraph* as the unit of perception and meaning. This is the "experience chart" on the wall of the classroom. Experience, however, tells anyone that we do not begin by reading a paragraph as a whole, and although the experts have not foregone the theory, they have generally in practice taken the sentence as the real unit of beginning learning. Children are asked to "frame" the sentence that says, "We baked a cake" and learn it as a whole. This too is a pious and ritualistic gesture, for again it is obvious that there is no future in framing whole sentences. So they go on to the word, and there they stop, for words *can* be taught as units. Letters are units, too, and have been units of perception, on blocks, to millions of children. A letter can be seen and learned in a way that fulfills all the Gestalt formulations about learning by units; but the experts advise against teaching the alphabet at home, and they refrain from teaching it to first-graders.

To return for a moment to an earlier illustration: telegraphy is a skill of turning one set of symbols into another set of symbols; the good telegraphist does this with ease, speed, and accuracy; when he has become expert he can do it with little thought or attention: he can send a message while carrying on a conversation. He is trained to this skill simply by drill, beginning with the letters, working with them until they come naturally to him, and at the same time varying the learning process by working with small groups of letters, until the skill becomes automatic and rapid. He does not have to be motivated by a discussion of the purpose of telegraphy; he does not have to be told a story or given experience; he does not have to "send for meaning" or "receive for meaning" before he fixes his attention on the code itself. He just has to drill on the skill until it becomes natural to him. *Then* his attention is released so that he can get the meaning of a message he is receiving.

In learning to read, the child needs a skill of turning letter-symbols into sound-symbols. This is first. It is basic. When he has this skill, be it ever so mechanical, he is ready to read for meaning. Being able to look at the print and *say* or know the sound of the word must precede getting its meaning, although the meaning may come almost simultaneously. When the child has mastered the skill he no longer thinks of it, just as the good adult reader does not have to think about sounding out a familiar word on a page. That skill has become so natural that he is no longer aware of it.

But beware of trying to skip this step. The look-and-say method tries to skip the basic, essential, mechanical—if you will—step of mastering the symbols so that they are used naturally and without thought or effort. Today we have in our high schools thousands of boys and girls who, given a nonsense word like *pim* or *galp* or *abt* or *erven* or *klor,* will look at it long and hard before coming out with an incorrect pronunciation.[4] These youths have not learned the code. They should be able to say these nonsense words *instantly,* without thought or effort, after the shortest possible glance at them. That is the skill upon which reading for meaning rests. The schools have not taught it. They are not teaching it.

The same motive of skipping the drill for quick and easy rewards underlies modern schemes of teaching piano by starting the pupil right in playing tunes—skipping thereby

[4] See the remarkable evidence on pp. 145–146 (Chapter X).

the dull drudgery of practicing scales. By this method, presumably, the pupil would later deduce the scales from the pieces he could perform. But musicians assure us that there is no substitute for the discipline of mastering the scales—and that pupils who begin by this short-cut method never become pianists. The parallel here between look-and-say reading and this sort of piano instruction is very close.

Six / A Further Look at Current Theory
and Its Logic

I am student-teaching in junior high school. . . . Reading is a fantastic problem! I have a boy with whom I am doing remedial reading work. The teacher has this boy read from the same page every day until he memorizes the words. When I first heard him read, I wondered that there was a problem at all. I thought he read beautifully. Then I turned to another page in the back of the book and asked him to read. He couldn't read one word! So, approaching the problem from what seemed a logical beginning, I wrote down the first 5 letters of the alphabet and taught him their sounds. Then we made up nonsense words— deb, ceb, bec, *etc. He asked me "Are these words I'm saying?" I told him no. Then I gave him* bed. *He responded, "Oh, that's what you sleep on." I was encouraged and continued with my process. The teacher called me aside at the end of the period and told me that I had been wasting my time. She told me that the phonic approach was the wrong one—that the boy's I.Q. was too low for that. This seemed the height of absurdity to me. Isn't it easier to memorize 26 sounds than hundreds of words?*

(Another letter from a former student)

WHOLES OR PARTS?

The first half of this chapter is for readers who would like to pursue somewhat further the implications of the theory of sight reading and perhaps for some who are not completely satisfied by the explanations in Chapter 5. It has to do largely with perception—how we see and how we learn to see in order to become fast and accurate readers. We are especially concerned to analyze some of the reasoning and some of the analytic method employed by educationists. We hope that scientists and businessmen, who are scrupulously careful about the accuracy and responsibility of whatever formal statements they make, and who tend to assume comparable care in others, will want to have more of the evidence upon which we have based our assertions that the educationists are not scientific and frequently not accurate in their statements of "fact."

According to the educationists' conception of Gestalt theory, perception begins with wholes and proceeds to discriminate the parts. Words must be seen as wholes for fast reading. Look-and-say begins with wholes for this reason and also because such learning is psychologically "right." This is the theory. But the facts are exactly the opposite. The authors learned to read by first learning the alphabet, then the sounds, then the nature of syllables, then words; we learned very quickly and easily. And we know that we see words as wholes, as do the many good adult readers whom we have consulted.

When we learn a new word today, we study it first by letters or syllables and thereby learn a total image of the word which serves us thereafter. Then when we "see" this word we are really recognizing a sound-image that is already in our minds, in full detail—which is a very different process from perceiving a complex new configuration, made of unfamiliar elements, for the first time, and not even knowing that it represents a sound. The difference between the almost instantaneous recognition of a familiar word and the perception of a totally new configuration is tremendous.

We learn our perfect image of a new word fairly easily because we are so familiar with the letters. We definitely do not see the word *elephant* as having a trunk and a tail; we do *not* recognize *cat* by the ears on the *t* or by the way the *c* opens its mouth toward the *a*. We do not have to notice the particular feature which distinguishes *horse* from *house*. We do not see the outlines or shapes of words. Nor, thank heaven, did we learn them that way.

Our problem readers who have been trained by look-and-say unfortunately do all these things. They look at the first letter or the first syllable of a word and blurt out a guess that does not resemble the whole word. They see *collection* and say *collision*. They hesitate and stumble and then build a wrong reading out of some syllable they have identified in the middle of a word. They have tricks for remembering words, and these tricks often betray them; for example, children in a second grade described to us were taught to remember *purple* by the two similar lines projecting below the word. When they saw the word *people* some time later, these children, if they remembered what they had been taught, would say *purple*. They would not see either word as a whole because they had actually been taught from the beginning to look at special parts of it in a special way. And this way, despite everything the theorists say, is a very bad way that must be unlearned if the child is ever to see words properly. But when a child learns something like this at the age of six or seven he has been taught a habit that may stay with him for years. Years later he may include those two projecting lines in his reaction to the word *purple,* and it may constitute an interference in his recognition of *people.*

To illustrate the mixture of incidental phonics with various other clues for word recognition now used in schools, we offer the following passage from a new defense of current practice by two professors:

Ann, who has been interested by the lesson on boats, has taken a book which was suggested by the teacher from the class library. In it there is a page with the sentence, "The ship sails on the water." The picture above this sentence shows a ship. Ann knows all the words except the new word "ship." Her first impulse is to say: "the *boat* sails on the water." This would be the logical result if the picture clue were used as the exclusive means of attacking the strange word. In fact, however, the *"o-a-t"* family of words has been so well learned by Ann that she instantly discards this word. Using both the picture clue and the context clue furnished by the familiar words in the balance of the sentence, Ann realizes that the word *ship* is another word for *boat*. Not knowing any synonym for *boat*, she is temporarily at a loss and asks the teacher for help. On many occasions the teacher will simply tell a child what such a word is so that the continuity of what she is reading will not be broken. In this particular instance, the teacher feels that she should take the time to help Ann attack this word. "Do you remember," she asks, "the letter we wrote to Rose the other day?" "Yes," says Ann, "we told her we were sorry that she had broken her hip."

Now, the teacher writes the word *hip*, which is immediately recognized by Ann. The next step is obvious. The *s* and the word *hip* are combined and Ann has the satisfaction of using picture clue, context clue, and phonics to figure out the unfamiliar word.[1]

We wonder what the teacher would have done if nobody had broken a hip lately. If this child really knew her letters and their basic combinations, she would have said *ship* at a glance. For in phonics *s-hip* does not make *ship*. The *sh* sound is a different sound and it must be taught as a unit. All this groping around to *guess* a word with three sets of clues—here is confusion confounded. There is a basic inertia about human beings, and a college student seared by this method will, rather than go through these shenanigans, just skip the word he doesn't recognize—and this is what an alarming number do today. They skip words they have seen hundreds of times. They are baffled by familiar words at which they always have to stop and think.

To show to what lengths the theorists will go to avoid

[1] Duker and Nally, *The Truth about Your Child's Reading*, p. 92.

teaching the alphabet specifically, we transcribe the following:

> If such confusions as *can-car, train-three, can-ran, ran-run,* or
> *play-played* occur, they suggest the need on the part of some
> children for help in noting the features which differentiate words,
> such as differences in configuration and general shape, in larger
> components and in letter composition or sequence. For example,
> the confusion between *can* and *car* must be cleared up by notic-
> ing the difference in the last letter.[2]

Notice again the analytic approach to these words: the child
is asked to learn them as wholes and later is led to look into
their details and find phonic elements and other clues for
distinguishing them. If the child knew the alphabet initially
and knew how these words were made to stand for *sounds,*
he would not become confused among them and he would
not have to be further confused by these laborious methods
of discriminating them. The whole difficulty is created by
the modern method of teaching.

FURTHER FACTS OF PERCEPTION

The educationists observe, correctly, that a good reader
sees four or five words, almost instantly, at a single glance
(called a "fixation"). They conclude that because a good
reader can see several words at once he cannot possibly have
time to see all their details and he must therefore see only
their outlines or shapes. The conviction that perceiving a
word as a whole involves seeing it as a shape appears in the
phrases "total configuration" and "configuration clues" (in-
dicating tall letters and flat letters) that occur repeatedly in
the educationist literature on reading. We are enjoined not
to talk about letters and the alphabet because to see these

[2] Arthur I. Gates, in his manual for teachers using his primer, quoted by
Duker and Nally, p. 93.

elements in a word would require (they think) looking at all the details in a word instead of just looking at its outline or shape. This thinking appears when *man* is taught as a flat or rectangular word, and the tall letters in *tall* are used to identify it.

These assumptions, which underlie the whole-word and "configuration" approach, are explicitly stated in the following passage, in which the common sense of the unscientific layman is refuted and indeed chided.

Teachers have always had common-sense principles to go by, rules and sayings which they were sure contained the truth. It once seemed completely obvious, for example, that you have to read words before you can read sentences, and that the way to learn to read words is to learn letters first. No one questioned this.... This logic dominated the teaching of reading until the reading process was studied in the psychological laboratory. The psychologists who became interested in reading about fifty years ago set out to determine how people actually read. They found that good readers do not actually notice the letters or syllables that make up a word. The good reader takes in a whole word or phrase at a single glance, *recognizing it by its outline* [italics ours!]. . . .

Now we teach pupils to recognize short words as units from the very beginning. Sentences and short stories are introduced as soon as the pupil knows just a few words. Spelling-out and analysis of syllables used to be the beginning of instruction. Now they are taught later as reserve techniques, to be a "low gear" that the reader uses when he encounters a word that defies instant recognition.

. . . Not all statements that seem sensible hold up when examined by controlled research. The major task of educational psychology is to help teachers discard some of the "sensible" views that are really too limited or based on inaccurate observation. The principles of educational psychology are acceptable both to rigorous scientific test and to common sense.[3]

[3] Cronbach, *Educational Psychology*, Harcourt, Brace and Company, New York, pp. 13–15. See also p. 46, above.

Now here we are pretty close to the heart of the matter, and the layman does not have to go into the laboratory to discover the innocent inference that has so completely misled the educational psychologists. He has merely to think for a moment about what happens when he reads familiar words rapidly. (Nobody can read unfamiliar words rapidly.) Suppose he reads "a conservative Republican Congressman." Does he see these words as outlines or shapes? No. Does he have to look at every letter in each word? Of course not. For he already has a full image of each word in his mind that he "sees" instantly when he takes in several words at a glance. He doesn't have to look at each letter on the page because the *full image of the word* is already stored in his brain. This is how we recognize (*not* perceive) words, not by their outlines or by configuration clues. *How* the brain calls up this total image we don't know, but it does. And it is obvious that it has to *have* the total image, with all its letters, before it can be evoked by the rapidly moving eye. We doubt that the outline of a word is a short cut to its recognition, or indeed that it even functions in rapid reading, because the image in one's brain is an image of the whole word. It is true that one can actually *see* only four or five random letters at a fixation, whereas a fast reader sees four or five words at a fixation, but this is because he has learned these words as wholes *with all their letters.* Everywhere in the educationist literature we come upon passages solemnly invoking such "scientifically established" facts about eye movements and yet quite unaware of the differences between (1) seeing a strange configuration, (2) memorizing a strange configuration, (3) seeing a word composed of familiar symbols, and (4) recognizing a word of which one has a complete and perfect mental image. The world is absolutely bulging with data and facts, but they are of no use unless they are correctly interpreted. The observation of Gestalt psychologists that we perceive wholes before we perceive the parts of which they are composed is here attached to these facts

70 CURRENT THEORY AND ITS LOGIC

of eye-movement—to produce a completely untenable theory of how a child should *learn* to read. We believe that this illogical union is the ultimate theoretical basis of the reading method that is today undermining our educational system. The prevalence of this theory appears in another recent expert book, where we read that "children and adults often recognize words quickly as wholes, and often recognize groups of words with rapidity, too. The good reader does not see each letter or all the letters. He may, for example, respond to the total form of the word and thus be aided in recognition of it," [4] and so on. This error is justified by the usual appeal to scientific research:

We teach pupils to recognize words as units from the very beginning. We do this because of demonstrated facts about the nature of perception. The letter is not the unit of perception in meaningful reading, as Gestalt psychologists have indicated repeatedly.[5]

No such facts can have been demonstrated because they are not facts. The question is not whether the letter is "the unit of perception in meaningful reading," but *how* do we learn and perceive a word?

A careful search through the literature has failed to discover *a single piece of research* which proves or even indicates that learning the letters before reading is a handicap. In spite of reiterated claims that current methods are based on scientific research, none seems to have been done on this cornerstone of educationist theory. The notion that teaching letters first will interfere with learning to read is an erroneous inference drawn from discoveries about eye-movements, not a proven fact.

We conclude that the children who learn to read well by

[4] Willard Abraham, *A New Look at Reading*, Porter Sargent, Boston, 1956, p. 12, from "An Interview with Paul A. Witty"—one of the deans of modern reading theory.
[5] *Ibid.*, p. 6.

look-and-say do so precisely because they ignore the "configuration clues" by which they are taught and get, from the beginning, mental images of whole words (undoubtedly because they already know the alphabet) that they can carry and use right through their lives. We believe that a good reader must know exactly what every word is made of, so that his mental image of it is reliable and definite. Only thus will he keep *mastic, mystic,* and *matrix* infallibly distinct when he is reading most rapidly. If he starts reading by guessing whether a word is *cow* or *man,* because both are small rectangles, he will never read well unless these shape clues are entirely washed from his mind.

The reader can test these statements easily by trying to memorize an Arabic word so that he can recognize it at a glance. If he does not know the Arabic alphabet, he will find it very difficult—if not impossible—just to *see* such a word at a glance; and it will be quite impossible for him to distinguish it from a number of words that are generally similar in size and shape. Imagine yourself an Arab trying to distinguish *wan* from *man* at a glance—and think how lost you would be if you did not know the letters *w* and *m* and the *sounds* they represent!

Anyone who can himself read will discover, on almost any page of Flesch's controversial book, that Flesch wants people to read with the utmost ease for the utmost intelligent *comprehension.* He has written a number of books on the art of communicating ideas accurately through the written word. His main concern is communication, and we repeat that this is so obvious that nothing would seem less necessary to point out. Yet nearly every answer to Flesch published accused him of regarding reading as merely pronunciation of words and said that he did not know we read for meaning. A recent one says, "Mr. Flesch regards reading as mere pronunciation of words. He does not seem to be interested in the meaning or the understanding of words." This misunderstanding of the problem appears in these sentences, a couple of pages farther:

> Moreover, it is abundantly clear that the letter combinations give us little or no clue as to meaning. Take the word "case." There are many meanings for this word: "I thought it was so, but it was not the case." "It was a case of bad judgment." "The judge tried the case." And so on.
>
> Now the meaning of this word comes from one's experience or from reading it in a meaningful context.[6]

Letter combinations make *sounds,* not meanings, and where a sound stands for several meanings there is of course still a problem. But these obvious facts have nothing to do with the simple question of whether the child can pronounce a printed word (or "sound") so that he can hear it and then perhaps find that he knows what it means. If you can read *c-a-s-e* and say "instance" you may be getting the meaning, but you are a very bad reader, and you are headed for trouble.

This astonishing distortion of Flesch continues. In a recent article, Albert J. Harris, president of the International Reading Association, comments on the fact that good readers take in several words at a single glance or "fixation," and continues:

> Flesch, on the other hand, just doesn't believe the results of these eye-movement studies, although he seems to have read about them. He says that one learns to become a fast reader by inspecting words letter by letter, with increasing speed. At this point he flatly denies a large and eminently respectable body of research data, because, presumably, it does not fit his theories. If fast readers do read letter by letter [*no one has ever said they do, although they may learn to read that way*], the intensive phonic method would be justified. Since they read by whole words and groups of words, the argument in favor of starting with whole words makes sense.[7]

[6] Abraham, *A New Look at Reading,* p. 6.
[7] "On Reading," *Spectrum,* II (Spring, 1957), p. 8.

It makes no sense at all; the two concluding sentences of this passage are not logical. How one reads is not how one learns to read. How one learns to read (by letters and syllables as sounds, if one learns well) is not how one reads when one is a mature reader. Here is the president of the International Reading Association dealing with the absolute core of this problem—and dismissing it in these few sentences.

FROM SPEED TO COMPREHENSION

How Do the "Good" Readers Read?

Our observation of college students is that a rather small fraction read really rapidly and that about 10 per cent read very slowly and laboriously. Research studies in the past have put the average speed at 250 words per minute. But we find that many facile and rapid readers do not and apparently cannot read for depth. These students appear to be "ideal" products of current look-and-say instruction. They have been trained to read for speed in readers with controlled vocabularies, going over the same words again and again until they can take them in with impressive ease and pace. Recall that the Fifth Reader, a fat 400-page volume, has a total vocabulary of 3,248 words. The student who has learned successfully by look-and-say can achieve tremendously through this drill.

But what the system does not seem to consider is that a really good reader has to surmount two or more major hurdles in his development. Somewhere in or just before his 'teens he has to take a giant step from stories to prose that deals with complex ideas in a vocabulary of abstractions. At this point the need is for precise vocabulary rather than speed. Speed, indeed, is a handicap when the ideas reach a certain density. A second major hurdle comes (rather, it should come) toward the end of high school, when the student passes on to writings of social and even philosophical theory—and poetry—that demand closer attention, still more vocabulary, and a deliberate ratiocinative approach. Here again speed is of less than no use. One must think about every sentence and linger over many words, for such writing deals with new worlds of thought that are not to be won without sustained effort. Now we know that the big national achievement tests undertake to test comprehension, and we know that many studies have "demonstrated" that the rapid readers understand as much as or considerably more than the slow ones, but these tests reward facility and superficiality rather than depth and imagination. We have seen this fact proved, and we have heard a testing specialist say, "Of course that is what the tests show, because that is what the schools ask for."

But to return to our hurdles: the fact is that most students do not appear to have surmounted them. They have not been required to do enough difficult reading. There has not been systematic, concentrated work on vocabulary. Indeed it appears that in many high schools the reading requirements become slighter during the two final years. Emphasis has been on "creativity" rather than on discipline, on general idea rather than precise meaning. These students are usually helpless before a poem because they have been taught that a poem is not to be read but "interpreted"; that is, it is to be given any meaning the student chooses to give it! Genuine bewilderment greets the college English instructor who says that poetry is the most precise form of communication through words and that it must be studied with the closest possible attention to the exact verbal meanings it is made of. With Carlyle, Mill, Huxley, Ruskin, Hume, or Locke one has to carry the average college student along sentence by sentence or he will find himself conducting a lively discussion that has nothing to do with the content of the essay being examined.

Thus, having produced some facile readers of easy prose, the schools have too often left them in this condition because their philosophies do not allow for hard work on thought-packed prose. Irrefutable evidence for these contentions can be found in the revisions of widely used high-school texts published during the past fifteen or twenty years. In almost every instance the revision simplifies the sentences, reduces the vocabulary, and attenuates the thought until there is not a really meaty sentence to be found on a page.

The sequence from a look-and-say beginning, through speed training with controlled-vocabulary readers, to adult reading that cannot cope with complex or thought-laden prose is, we believe, a *causal* sequence; and its very disturbing consequences are college admission and achievement examinations which demonstrably and admittedly favor the facile student (who is in the overwhelming majority) while they confuse the thoughtful one.

We have mentioned the dominating concepts in the teaching of primary reading, the stress on reading for meaning, on experience, motivation, reading readiness, and the needs of each individual child.

These notions prevail through the secondary grades in three parallel forms which we must now examine if we are to see why our "good" high-school readers do not read with understanding.[8]

1. *The Theory of Conceptual Reading.* This notion goes back at least as far as 1908, when a book by Edward Burke Huey entitled *The Psychology and Pedagogy of Reading* presented the theory that thinking begins with a concept or total idea and that words follow the idea. Thus he says that emphasis should be on the total idea rather than on the individual words in a sentence. Mr. Huey argues that the total meaning can be grasped (approximately, and he says that is all that matters) even though the reader does not know all the words. Nor is what the author said so important as what the author *suggests to the reader.* For this reason, Mr. Huey

[8] What follows on this topic is summarized from an unpublished address by Professor George Sensabaugh to the Stanford University Alumni Association.

argues that a child may even substitute "words of his own for some that are on the printed page, provided that these express the meaning." Reading is *not* saying what is on the printed page but *thinking* "the meaning that the page suggests." This will differ for each reader because "reading is always of the nature of translation and, to be truthful, must be free ... and until the insidious thought of reading as word-pronouncing is well worked out of our heads, it is well to place the emphasis strongly where it really belongs, on reading as *thought-getting*, independently of expression."

From this theory we get loose reading that is more likely to discover what is in the student's mind already than what the author has put on the printed page. How far Mr. Huey's 1908 volume has shaped practice during the past thirty years would be hard to determine; but it is clear that his theories are reflected in current practice wherever we have observed it. Close, precise reading cannot flourish under this theory.

2. *The Doctrine of Immediacy.* This extends the theoretical stress on experience. It maintains that the reading program must be closely related to the immediate problems of the students' lives. It must deal with the world they know and the problems they face in the immediate present. A National Council of Teachers of English commission, in a volume entitled *The English Language Arts* (Appleton-Century-Crofts, Inc.), elaborates this notion. It proposes curriculum-making that does not list topics to be mastered but attempts "to define maturing powers to be attained in thinking, speaking, listening, writing, and reading, and to relate them constantly to the problems of living in a democracy today." [9] Thus "where instruction is given to meet genuine needs" it will be through a curriculum formulated around such units as "Living in a World of Advancing Science," or "Living in an Air Age." [10] If these units do not include the classics of our cultural heritage, the classics must go.

[9] P. 15.
[10] Pp. 113, 123.

It is plain that such a program can put little stress on careful, precise reading of great literary works, for such works are far from the "immediate" problems of living in an air age. And even when these units are supplemented by readings in stories and poems, the emphasis on "sharing experiences" would seem to preclude careful analysis and close, responsible reading of exact meanings, for it is the students' problems and reactions that are to be shared rather than the precise meaning of what some antique author chose to write down in another era when problems were "different." Even when major classics are included in these programs, they are scanned for general ideas and contemporary relevance rather than studied closely to find exactly what they say. This doctrine, then, reflects and extends the primary-school emphasis on experience. It assumes that children do not learn from books but are stimulated by them to explore their own problems. A recent text in educational psychology deplores the fact that so much great literature deals with the lives of kings and heroes—not with characters into whom the typist or clerk can project an image of himself and his very limited existence. It is not good, apparently, for the typist to be disturbed by images of lofty greatness in tragic conflicts. These will not help her adjust to her inglorious life.[11] If the schools do not want to disturb simple people with the lives of kings and heroes, it is not surprising that they should not want to disturb them with serious thought.

3. *The Fetish of Personality* answers to the early stress on motivation and "reading readiness." It distorts a respect for the individual into an exaggerated notion of individualism. The National Council of Teachers of English commission mentioned above, for example, says that where the needs of the individual are paramount, grades, standards, and nonpromotion become more or less irrelevant. Hence the curriculum should include no list of required readings for the high-school student. The material to be read "should be

[11] Cronbach, *Educational Psychology*, p. 323.

determined by the needs of the learners. The important consideration is the value of a selection to an individual student —the extent to which it contributes to his insights into his own behavior and that of others, and the extent to which it promotes in him a value system consonant with the ideals of a democratic society." [12]

These are but wild and whirling words that we cannot stop to analyze. We would merely ask how the "needs" of the individual student are to be discovered. How is the teacher indoctrinated with this idea to determine whether Joe Zooks in the back row of her large class "needs" Shakespeare or Milton—or just Miltown? And what does she know about the relation between Homer and "a value system consonant with the ideals of a democratic society"? Our Founding Fathers saw the closest relations between the classics and the ideal citizen of a republic. Jefferson wrote at considerable length on the subject. Today, the "needs"—the unknowable "needs" of the obscure student—are presumed to outweigh the values in the classics. And again, when this sort of random and irresponsible selection of reading material is practiced, it is plain that little attention can be given to the analysis of literary subtleties. "If the classics stand in the way of vital education, so much the worse for the classics."

Thus the theory of conceptual reading, the doctrine of immediacy, and the fetish of personality combine during the secondary-school years to keep the students' reading easy, general, vague, escapist, and superficial. The student who has survived the look-and-say beginning and become a rapid reader is protected through high school from the responsible or disciplined reading of difficult writing, for in these theories reading is not really taken very seriously. Activities, group planning, and discussion dominate today whereas in the past it was the printed word that was the staple and focus of learning.

[12] Pp. 194–195.

Seven / Some Social and Emotional
Consequences

We have speculated that an inhibiting emotional disturbance may set in when the child is asked to make a transition from one way of looking at printed words to another—from seeing them as wholes that *mean* to seeing them as made up of letters that represent sounds. Of course, if the child knew the alphabet, this step would never have to be made, because the knowledge that letters (and therefore printed words) were sounds would have been implicit in the whole learning experience from the very beginning.

The child who has learned in an uncertain manner to read fifty or a hundred and fifty sight words is then taught a few initial consonant sounds. Somehow the sound of *b*, *c*, or *d* at the beginning of a word is supposed to help tell him what the word says. It does not, however, because the clue is inadequate. It just adds to his confusion. This new difficulty, added to those he has been struggling with, may be the last straw. He may suddenly withdraw from the whole problem in what appears to be a condition of despair. The child must have known some sight words in order to experience this shock; yet when he has become a nonreader we find that he has forgotten all the sight words he ever knew; he has come to a state where he cannot read anything at all, although he may be ten or twelve years old and have been suffering exposure to school and remedial-reading instruction for five or six years.

Such forgetting is not remarkable. Adults who can remember dozens of telephone numbers or addresses find that they forget these numbers completely when they cease to use them. There is even more motive for forgetting with the frustrated child. When he reaches the point where he cannot cope with the reading process, he proceeds to forget every word he has known. Whereas once he could read sentences in the controlled vocabulary of his primer, now he has responded to bafflement by losing the ability to identify a single word.

Nonreaders of this extreme kind are rare but familiar to every experienced remedial teacher. They come to her with their desperate parents, who may already have been to school, doctor, psychologist, and reading clinic. It appears that their child is incapable of reading anything. The tension in the family is fearsome to behold. Yet a new remedial teacher may be able to gain the child's confidence and cooperation, restore his belief that he can learn, and by introducing him to the simplest beginnings of phonics, get him started reading again, and the results sometimes seem miraculous.

We have heard a reading expert explain, in a public speech, that substantially all reading problems are due to prior psychological maladjustments in the children. We have seen the same reason given varying degrees of emphasis in many articles on the problem. Emotional disturbance is set forth as a basic cause in almost every book by an educationist on the reading problem during the past fifteen or twenty years.

Remedial-reading teachers have, on the other hand, worked with problem readers who were having serious emotional difficulties and whose difficulties disappeared when their reading problems were solved. Which was cause and which was effect?

We believe the explanation of these facts is to be found in the literature of the conditioned response, particularly in Pavlov's work on experimentally produced neuroses. The great Russian psychologist Pavlov discovered in a classic experiment that by ringing a bell whenever a dog was given food he could so condition the dog that he would, after a time, salivate merely when the bell was rung.

He also found how to produce a nervous breakdown in a dog or a rat. The procedure was to present the dog with an ellipse and a circle in such a manner that the dog had to distinguish between them in order to get at his food. The dog can make this distinction successfully and act upon it; he is a well-adjusted dog! Then the experimenters proceed, diabolically, to alter the ellipse by degrees so that it very slowly approaches the shape of the circle. There comes the time, inevitably, when the dog can no longer distinguish between the two figures, and when this happens he has a nervous breakdown and loses the ability to make discriminations which he was earlier able to make. He may go into sullen retirement; he may whine, shiver, and moan; the rat under comparable provocation reacts dramatically: he may have convulsions; he may become hysterical and go into tantrums of fury. After this experience the dog has to be given a long rest, with care and affection, to bring him back to normality. (Rats are expendable.)

The child whose reading is retarded goes through the same cycle. He has learned to recognize a number of words by sight in his primer. So long as his memory keeps up with the words that he has to know he is successful and adjusted. But when the new words come faster than he can remember them, or, more typically, when the phonic clues that are introduced interfere with the habits of word-recognition he is employing, then he finds himself in the situation of the dog when the ellipse is every day becoming more like the circle. And his response is similar. He sulks, he withdraws into himself, may hate school, fear his teachers, and quarrel with his schoolmates. The real trouble is that he is confronted with new demands which he is not capable of meeting. He can't make the required discriminations; he is forced to work at a problem with no solution and is punished for failure. If the frustration reaches a certain point the child ceases to try, and the deterioration of both his reading and his personal adjustment may from that point be very rapid.

Now for a very important point. When this sort of child is retrained in phonics by an experienced remedial teacher, so that he gets the reading KEY and suddenly finds himself, his emotional problems vanish as if by magic. Dr. Orton has pointed out that the typical disturbed children with reading difficulties were happy and well-adjusted before the reading problem arose. Fernald has made the same observation.[1] Successful remedial teachers report again and again that the greatest reward in their work is seeing the unhappy maladjusted child begin to gain confidence, open up, and forget his fears. But *if the emotional disturbance had preceded the reading difficulty* and therefore caused it, it would not disappear merely because the reading problem was corrected. Persons with deep-seated neuroses that go back to disturbances in early childhood can learn to read, if taught properly (and often even though taught improperly), but learning to read does not cure their neuroses.

There is another reason for the child's withdrawing his attention from the reading lesson: the material bores him. The bright child, who has learned new words easily, sometimes cannot force himself to pay attention to subject matter suitable to a three-year-old. When we recall the romance and adventure of reading when we were children, the excitement of a rainy afternoon, of reading in bed after the light was supposed to be out, of living for days in the world of D'Artagnan, Penrod, Monte Cristo—so that the world around us seemed a dream—it is heartbreaking to look at the steri-

---

[1] Orton, *op. cit.* Fernald, *Remedial Techniques in Basic School Subject*, McGraw-Hill Book Company, Inc., New York, 1942, p. 8.

lized pap which is supposed to nourish the young today. Following the established program, your child does not read literature; he reads versions which have been rewritten so that they will have the proper vocabulary. This stuff is so unbelievably unliterary that you have to read it yourself to find how bad it is.

Being forced into a boring situation day after day is just as great a frustration as failing day after day and can produce similar nervous and rebellious reactions. A generation ago we read the classics at ten, like other children. We remember living in these books for days at a time, so eager to get back to them that we bolted our food and rushed from the dining table with no word for the family. Today *The Count of Monte Cristo* has been rewritten, not for ten-year-olds, but for junior-high-school and high-school students whose reading skills limit them to this sort of thing, into a book scarcely a twentieth the size of the original, and this is the way it goes:

In the morning Edmond filled his pockets with treasure. Then he left the cave. He hid the entrance with rocks and bushes. No one could tell that the cave was there.

Now he could hardly wait for the ship to come back. He wanted to get back to the world. He had many plans.

The ship came back on the sixth day. The sailors were glad to find Edmond so much better. They took him back to Italy. There he left the ship.

This horrible stuff is not prose by any measure. It is a series of stiff, declarative, simple sentences, without grace, imagination, or insight. Note the harsh repetition of the word *back*. Note the absence of the least shred of rhythm, humor, imagination—of anything that would make a curious kid want to read. How could anyone find this stuff compelling? How could a ten-year-old have any feeling but disgust for it? How can a high-school student take it seriously? If this is the price of learning to read, one might as well stay illiterate, and many do.

Nor have we chosen here to display a uniquely gross example. This outrage has been committed in the same style on a *list* of fine books which should be treasures of delight and adventure for our young, because there is a tremendous demand for them by retarded high-school students.

The regular school readers are no better. Think of your own secret life when you were ten or eleven. Recall the sensitivity, the imagination, the vivid awareness you had then, and consider that at about twelve this would have been considered pretty stiff going for you:

One of the first things you learn as you start growing up is that all food must be clean. Your mother puts no vegetables or fruits on the table which have not been washed carefully. You think of such behavior as usual among human beings. But did you know that there is a fairly common neighbor of the woods and fields who is nearly as careful as you are about having food clean?

This comes toward the end of a Fifth Reader, which is read by about half of our sixth-graders in America. By the time the twelve-year-old has read through 454 pages of stuff like this (or worse) he will be handling a vocabularly of 3,248 words—which is probably fewer words than he knew when he was four. There is no beauty, no grace, no style, no thrill in 454 pages of this. Certainly there can be no linguistic excitement, because the same poor words are repeated and repeated until they are worn bare. Many children of this age could be reading Cooper or Scott, authors whom one will hardly turn to after he is thirteen or fourteen, at the oldest, although they use vocabularies far beyond what the current sixth-grader has been taught. But today there is "an effort to shield the child from reading material in which the content is not directly connected with firsthand experience,"[2] up through the fourth and possibly the fifth grade, with the exception of some fairy stories.

[2] Duker and Nally, *op. cit.*, p. 122.

A newspaper columnist writes with feeling about the quality of books he is asked to read to his children:

We loving parents can buy books for our children at almost every turn. We can find them for sale at cigar stands, supermarkets, hotel lobbies, railroad stations, and probably even in the bookstores. They are clearly printed, colorfully illustrated and modestly priced. But as something to read, they are almost entirely slop.

I find they are written by psychiatrists, psychologists, child-rearing experts, radio performers and television actors. In fact, they are written by just about everybody except writers.

These books are scientifically manufactured to brainwash the small children. Each volume has a mission. One tells the kids to love the postman. Another to love the policeman at the corner. A third to help with the dishes, or the garden, or some other unpleasant household chore.

In all of them mother and father are great, unerring personages who never do anything wrong, never frown or speak harshly even to a fly. Maybe that's why these books have such a great sale. They flatter us.

Such small advantage is clearly outweighed by the agony of having to read this drivel to the small ones. They will listen to anything because they don't know any better.

But the harm done lasts on, according to no less an authority than Mrs. Frances C. Sayers, formerly with the New York Public Library. She maintains this junk is one reason kids stop reading books after they leave school.

I found a white-haired clerk at a local bookstore who has solved my problem. She now sells me nothing that isn't old enough to have been read to me in my early youth. The books are intelligent, amusing, literate and completely nonscientific. The kids love them. So do I.[3]

In a frustrating situation when faced with a problem that has no answer, one type of child withdraws into himself, another becomes aggressive and rebellious. The latter type may become the delinquent adolescent. The following news-

[3] Abe Mellinkoff, "Bookworm Turns Back to His Youth," *San Francisco Chronicle,* August 9, 1956.

paper column by a psychologist points to a connection between the reading problem and delinquency. It is a phase of the problem that transcends many others in importance:

A college professor studied the reading ability of successful men. Can you guess what he found? He found they almost all were very good readers. Doctors, lawyers, businessmen, engineers, scientists, teachers. They read rapidly. They comprehended what they read. They remembered what they had read.

I've been comparing the reading ability of that successful group with the reading ability of a gang of unsuccessful adults. My group contains both men and women. They all are delinquent. Their crimes run from petty theft to murder.

Can you guess what I've found about their reading? My group members all are poor readers. Some of them are bright, some are dull. Some are fat, some are lean. Some came from rich homes, some from poor ones. They have but one characteristic in common. They read slowly, stumblingly, without comprehension and without remembering what they've read. The difference between the groups is clear-cut and decisive. This does not mean that good readers don't ever become delinquent. A few do. And it doesn't mean poor readers are bound to become delinquent. Not that. Many poor readers are good citizens.

But the comparison does point up the importance of reading. I am convinced that poor reading ability is one of the things that cause people to go bad. They fail at school. They get rebellious. They play hooky. They gang up. Then they turn to crime as their natural outlet. It's a cause-and-effect relationship in many cases.[4]

The idea that failure in reading is a contributing cause of juvenile delinquency is widely accepted. The school people agree but claim that they have tried their best to teach reading and that the delinquent boys are *incapable* of learning.

To account for the greater number of boys than girls who fail at reading, let us consider some findings about sex dif-

[4] Richmond Barbour, "Poor Reading Ability Often Causes Delinquency in Men," Palo Alto *Times*.

ferences. They will explain also the tendency for the non-reading boy to become delinquent. It has been observed that, at primary-school age, girls are more docile, more willing to learn, less inclined to ask questions, more easily satisfied with purely formal activities. Boys are less docile; they are better than girls at problems that demand "restructuring" rather than the application of simple techniques; they are more aggressive, less patient, more inclined to conduct that emphasizes their individuality. The brighter the boy the less willing he will be to conform to a situation that does not appeal to him as reasonable. Boys are better in mathematics, girls in language.

Some psychologists now doubt that these differences are inherent or inherited; rather they are learned; they reflect what society expects of boys and girls. But nevertheless they exist, and they bear on the reading problem. Girls are willing to learn by routine memorization. Boys are inclined to ask questions and are attracted by problems that appeal to their reasoning abilities. They want to lead, to *manage,* and the control of a problem or situation by the use of the reason is a prime means of satisfying this need.

In the classroom, the little girl appears to be willing to learn one word after another by rote. The boy in the same situation is bored; he wants a challenge; he wants some approach through which he can use his reasoning powers. We know from experience that such a boy would be attracted by reading if he were given the phonic key and allowed to apply it in problem-solving situations from which he could get the satisfaction that comes with accomplishment. But if his aggressive characteristics are strong, such a boy will quickly become restless and unruly under the boredom of the protracted repetition that goes with the teaching of reading today. When he gets behind the others, he tends to become more unruly, seeking to get the attention by misbehaving that he is not able to get by outstanding accomplishment. It will not take very much of this sort of conduct to put the boy in a situation of failure and shame that will create a deep-seated antagonism to reading. When this has happened, we have a boy who will do poorly in school.

We have evidence that the schools today tend to give up on boys who don't learn to read in the first three or four years. They conclude that they have "specific reading disability" (i.e., cannot be taught to read) and devote their efforts to more rewarding children. As soon as a boy with strong instincts toward self-expression finds himself out of the main stream of schoolwork he is going to become increasingly frustrated and difficult.

Juvenile delinquency has been receiving a good deal of attention recently in New York City, where the concentrated population has made its incidence more alarming than it is elsewhere in the country. Over and over again those in authority have pointed out that reading retardation goes hand in hand with truancy, school failure, and juvenile delinquency. A report to Mayor Wagner by Deputy Mayor Henry Epstein, 1955, says that "failure in reading accounts more than any other single factor for behavior problems, truancy, and general school failure."

To end this chapter on a brighter note—all the teachers using the new methods of teaching reading, upon which we shall report in detail in Chapter 10, have made a special point of describing the happiness and good behavior, the alertness, respectfulness, and responsibility of children in their classes. It seems highly unlikely that such happy and productive children will become delinquents. They certainly will not become nonreaders, because they are reading in the first grade. It does not seem extravagant to expect that better teaching of reading will cause a substantial reduction of juvenile delinquency.

Eight / Science and Mythology in
Current Theory

A moot word in the reading controversy is "scientific," along with its cousin "research." Every piece of writing on the subject by a reading specialist invokes, at some time, like a knight in shining armor, the glowing figure of Science, holding in its triumphant hand the bright sword of Truth. As they see it, Science works through research and reaches conclusions that are verified and infallible. We have found that wherever the educationists run head-on into a statement that questions one of their basic convictions their answer includes a positive reference to the research that has scientifically proved their point.

We should like to explain the scientific method, for we have found that it is frequently invoked by people who do not understand it. How does a scientist who knows his business attack a piece of research? He does *not* begin by assembling data. He begins with a *problem*—a phenomenon in the world of fact whose cause and nature he wishes to establish accurately enough so that he can control it and/or predict what will happen when certain elements are added or taken away. Mere phenomena do not constitute a subject. There must be something about which the scientist wants to formulate an *explanatory* statement to account for how the facts in the observed situation function as they do.

Beginning, then, with a phenomenon that he wants to explain, the scientist looks at facts related to the phenomenon and formulates a *hypothesis,* which is a statement of the relation of the facts to the phenomenon. It may be a guess, an inspired insight, or an explanation of which the scientist is definitely suspicious. The greatest scientists have generally made their greatest discoveries through hypotheses that were inspired insights. When Albert Einstein, for example, came downstairs one day from his study and said to his wife, "Mother, I have just made a nice little equation," his $E = mc^2$ was such an insight. Such guesses are the outstanding events in the history of science.

The second step in the scientific method is the testing of the hypothesis by experiment under controlled conditions. Sustained, meticulous observation of data determines whether the hypothesis does indeed explain all the phenomena related to the problem. When the research scientist comes upon instances where his hypothesis does not account for the facts, he reviews and probably alters the hypothesis. He must have the hypothesis to orient and direct his researches, but he is continually ready to modify it as he discovers its inadequacies. The hypothesis is the key. When it is as great as Einstein's $E = mc^2$, it has directed the researches of a generation of scientists without being altered (so far as we know) at all. It has enabled astronomers, while verifying it, to solve a centuries-old mystery as to the exact position of the planet Mercury; it has guided the research which devised the atomic bomb and developed nuclear energy. Other hypotheses, at the opposite end of the scale, collapse under testing and have to be radically modified or completely abandoned. If the ultimate greatness of scientists lies in their inspired guesses, close behind come the method and the patience to test these guesses and the objectivity which enables them to abandon their hypotheses when they do not stand up.

Religion and mythology operate differently from science,

for they begin with a "revealed" or inspired or uncriticized "truth" to which the facts must be related. They begin with definitions and dogmas to which people are so emotionally committed that they *serve* them rather than scrutinize them. When a Christian theologian, for example, works out a logical proof of the existence of God, he is not setting out to test the hypothesis but to prove it. He knows it must be true, or he would not be a Christian theologian; his intellectual researches are directed toward finding proof for what he believes through deep and earnest faith.

This is proper for religion, but it is an attitude which unfortunately has operated through the whole history of human thought to interfere with the discovery of truth. The belief of the Classical world that matter was composed of four elements—earth, fire, air, and water—served for centuries, indeed for millenia, as a convenient hypothesis in terms of which physical science could arrange and explain its data. Controlling the frame of reference as it did, it of course prevented the observation (let alone the analysis) of facts which could not be reconciled to it. This great hypothesis was transferred from physical to human nature, and the constitution of man was defined as consisting of four *humours* corresponding to the four elements. These were cold, hot, dry, and wet, embodied in phlegm, yellow bile (choler), black bile (melancholy), and blood. The proportions of these humours were believed to determine an individual's temperament and health, and medicine was controlled by the frame of reference that they constituted. If a fact did not fit into this frame, it was ignored; if a theory ran head-on into it, it was violently rejected.

The physical sciences have one by one got free from such mythological hypotheses, but never without a struggle, and the struggle is never completely won. We know that Copernicus was denounced for asserting that the earth revolves around the sun; that Jenner was vilified by the medical profession for his work with inoculation for smallpox; that late in the nineteenth century Semmelweis, who demonstrated that puerperal fever was carried from one mother to another in a hospital ward on the hands of the doctor, could not persuade doctors to wash their hands between patients—even when these patients were dying of puerperal fever by scores and hundreds. A hypothesis often carries a sort of enchantment with it, for it satisfies the human need for simplicity and pattern; and so people are most unwilling to abandon it. They have in scores of historical instances gone through incredible difficulties to justify a hypothesis which to an unprejudiced observer would appear to be no longer defensible. The experts come to identify themselves emotionally with the hypothesis to which they have given their time and their efforts.

This somewhat extended description of well-known facts has been given because it will help the layman grasp the situation that prevails with the reading problem. When the "expert" insists that he is right because he has devoted years of study to the subject, the layman can comfort himself with the thought that this expert may be mistaken for the very same reason. When he is confronted with mountains of books and articles (for instance a *selected* bibliography entitled *Eight More Years of Research in Reading* by Arthur Traxler and Agatha Townsend, 1955, listing nearly 800 studies published between 1945 and 1953), the layman may set this mass of research over against the too obvious fact that children are not learning to read well and conclude that such a massive accumulation represents an attempt to sustain an indefensible theory. When he is asked the indignant rhetorical question, "Do you think that *all* these devoted specialists can be mistaken?" he should not be afraid to consider the possibility that if they are emotionally committed to any central doctrine or body of doctrine they may indeed all be mistaken—and that in any event mere quantity of research on a subject has never guaranteed truth. It is a notable fact in the history of science that when an expert emphasizes his authority he does so because he is uncomfortable with hypotheses which are being challenged but which he does not wish to reconsider.

We shall try now to show that the reading specialists have proliferated a body of mythic lore inspired by the fact that reading has not been taught successfully by theories and methods which they are convinced *must work* if they are just tried hard enough. Let us examine some doctrines in this light:

Myth No. 1: A Variety of Methods, Causes, Symptoms

One of the most plausible and widespread legends in the mythology is the statement, "We do not restrict ourselves to any single method. We use the method that is best fitted to the needs and the personality of the individual child." This statement, in some form, appears literally hundreds of times in the literature. It comes up when one proposes a "phonic" approach, and it comes up whenever one suggests that "the present method" is faulty. "Oh, no," is the reply; "we don't have *a* method; we use the method which the teacher finds most appropriate to the individual child." We have seen (Chapter 3) the batteries of reasons given for reading difficulty and the description of "fifty tests and examinations" given to a problem reader.

This sounds so reasonable, so patient, so open-minded that it commands assent from almost anybody. A variety of methods, a complexity of causes—these phrases evoke stereotypes of scientific thoroughness and humane concern for individual differences.

But if the reader will turn back to the description of how reading is taught, in Chapter 4, he will see that there is just *one method*, not a variety, and that the prohibition on beginning with the alphabet is dogmatic and positive. The myth contradicts the facts. Furthermore, it is fascinating to observe that it is precisely because the most necessary detail is prohibited that the educationists are unable to diagnose reading retardation—and so instead of hitting on the single almost universal cause, namely, ignorance of the alphabet and the phonic element in reading, they offer a score of causes that miss the mark.

In speaking of college students who needed remedial reading, one author starts by making a list of the symptoms that these students displayed: they adopted a slow rate of reading, they could not adjust their rate to different types of material, they lacked accuracy, they comprehended little of what they read, they could not concentrate on difficult materials, they had poor vocabulary scores, they could not organize material, and they lacked an understanding of the precise meaning of many words. After making a careful case study of each student, the author gave them seven types of training: rapid reading of fairly easy interesting materials, leisure reading, speed reading practice, training in organizing short phrases on the tachistoscope, vocabulary building exercises, exercises to facilitate the mastery of skimming, reading for details and getting the general thought, help in reading textbooks. There were also frequent individual conferences. This is the type of work done in college reading clinics; it may result in improved reading. However the basic cause of these symptoms described is ignored. These students learned to read without a proper grounding in phonics. Books on the improvement of college reading commonly make no reference to the need for phonics training.

Yet look what some recent research shows. Two professors with years of experience with college reading problems have devised a group phonics test (described in detail in Chapter 10). Testing a large number of students in three colleges, they found that from 23 to 71 per cent had difficulty in reading words or nonsense syllables that were new to them. Students with low scores on this test exhibit all the difficulties described above. They are reading—and reading poorly—with words they know by sight, but because they have trouble with new words they are in constant difficulties, making guesses, going by context, missing the precise meaning again and again. What they need, of course, is some systematic drill in letters and sounds. The authors of this test have found that unless training in phonics is given first to those who need it, such exercises as those suggested above are apt to produce only a temporary improvement.

Myth No. 2: The Child or the Method?

Our position is that the *difficulties* in the process of learning to read which educationists think are *inherent in the learning process* and therefore characteristics of children, are in actual fact produced by the methods now used upon the child. These difficulties, therefore, need not occur at all under a more reasonable system, although they are treated as if they were facts of human nature. The myth again completely reverses the facts. Here are the sublegends of this myth:

1. *Left-to-right Confusions and Reversals.* Children whom we have observed to be properly taught have never displayed this confusion, although they were never specifically taught anything to prevent it. The child writing an S backward has usually not learned to write S correctly, but any four-year-old can be taught it in a few minutes. The child who confuses *saw* with *was* does so because the same letters are involved and he has not grasped the importance of saying the left-hand one first.

Confusions of *b* and *d* or *p* and *q* or *b* and *p* mean that the child has seen that these four letters are the same shape and has not grasped the fact that the position is important. In one direction there is a *b*; in another position the same thing is a *q*. Naturally he will not see the connections between sounds and letters until he gets the forms properly placed.

Reversals within a word are another matter. *An* is pronounced *na*, and *girl* is called *grill*. A child taught *an, ai, gr, ir*, as units with their own sounds could never make these mistakes. A high-school boy spelled *hens* "schen." He apparently confused the words *hens* with *chickens*. One small boy, innocent of the concept that words are sounded from left to right (and much confused in general), regularly looked as he had been taught to do, at the first letter and then at the last letter of a word, started with the sound of the last letter, since that is where he found himself, next read the first letter—and *trucks* was read as *struck*. This is a direct outgrowth of being started on configurations instead of letters.

The reading adult takes in a whole word in one "fixation." Read a line of this page backward, and you will find that you see the words as well and as fast as you do going in the right direction. This shows that *sounding* words from left to right is not spontaneous, not caused by natural eye movements. One does not automatically discover that words are *sounded* from left to right; he must be taught this fact or brought to words in such a way that he cannot get any other idea.

2. *Lack of Reading Readiness.* In children who are bright, well-behaved, and well-adjusted, there can be no such thing as lack of reading readiness if they are taught the letters and the sounds of the alphabet first. There is no such thing as a normal child who cannot learn the alphabet, though some will be slower than others. With the right method, reading readiness can infallibly be produced in a week. The failure of reading readiness in the bright child is, as shown in the study by F. T. Wilson, quoted by Paul Witty,[1] simply a failure to learn the first steps in reading—the letters and sounds— because they are kept from him by modern theory. The children who learn fast are those who have forestalled the system by learning the letters at home.

3. *"Specific Reading Disability."* There are normal children who after several years of school work have not made a beginning at reading. They occur in *all* progressive schools;

[1] *Reading and the Educative Process*, p. 181. See below, p. 105.

they are explained by the experts as children who inherently develop at a slower rate than others. This is a mistaken application of the doctrine of individual differences.

Textbooks on the teaching of reading agree that there are children with normal or high I.Q.s who have "a specific reading disability" and who must be taught by special methods or who can never be taught to read well. Yet many competent remedial-reading teachers of our acquaintance are convinced that virtually no such cases would come to light under a better system of instruction. Under the systems described in Chapter 10 and under the instruction of many individual teachers who begin with the alphabet, there have been large numbers of children learning to read in the first grade with no cases of failure.

4. *Aphasia.* This means "loss or impairment of the power to use or understand speech, resulting from brain lesion or, sometimes, from functional or emotional disturbance" (Webster's *New Collegiate*). Every remedial-reading teacher knows the really serious case of the child who just can't seem to *say* the word even though he recognizes the printed symbol. One boy, for example, always said, when he came to *until*, "Oh, there's that darn word again." Extreme cases can't seem to articulate any of the familiar words before them on the page. Some experts and doctors like to spot this condition and identify it with the word aphasia and tell you that it is a serious congenital abnormality. A good remedial-reading teacher recognizes it as a temporary and easily removed emotional block. It is simply another example of a disintegration of behavior under the pressure of fear and confusion, when the child is compelled to try to make discriminations for which he has not been prepared. The same child has no difficulty whatever in calling up the same words and using them freely in spoken sentences far more complicated than those he is asked to say when he has a book in his hand.

5. *Eye Movements.* A good deal of work, often with carefully devised instruments, has been devoted to the study of

eye movements. Performance charts are made in which the number of "fixations" per line is shown, along with the number of "regressions." These latter are glances back over the line to reread words already covered. The child who is told to look over a word and find a "clue," such as the two tall letters at the end, may make several fixations on a single word. Again, the trouble is not with the child's eyes but with the habits that have been established by these suggestions. This is what the child is taught to do, and it is all he is equipped to do, in the method that pretends to have him reading whole sentences at a glance. This makes him a laborious reader for the rest of his life. But the theorists cannot comprehend that there simply is no way to read a whole sentence fast until one knows all the words in it instantly.

Myth No. 3: English Is 13 per cent Nonphonetic

One of the commonest mythic defenses of the look-and-say method is the statement that "the English language is only 87 per cent phonetic." The statement is often followed by references to words like *through, dough, tough, psalm,* and so on, which we all know are irregular. The argument is that the phonic patterns which are regular run into the many exceptions and so confuse the learning child that he ceases to learn at all because he cannot find consistent patterns of sound in the letters of the words that he is learning. This sounds so clear and obvious that it has been repeated a thousand times in articles, books, and discussions. It is one of the unchallenged defenses of look-and-say. And yet the whole argument can be refuted quite simply. There are two points to make:

1. In the first place, it is not the English language that is 13 per cent nonphonetic. It is English spelling. This is a minor point but worth making in the interests of accuracy. We have looked far and wide to find what is meant by this

87 per cent figure, and the further we have looked the more divergent statements we have found.

We do not know whether the 87 per cent count considers word frequency or whether it is a figure based on the analysis of a large sample of English spellings, with each word counted once regardless of frequency. Nor do we know whether *said*, for example, with two proper letters and one very irregular combination (ai as short e) is nonphonetic or two-thirds phonetic. For these reasons we say that the statement "English is 87 per cent phonetic" is a mythic statement. Nobody seems to know what it means.

2. Our second point is startling, but the truth is that precisely *because* English spelling is frequently nonphonetic, it is essential to begin reading instruction with emphasis on basic phonic drill. This apparently wild statement makes sense when you consider that if English spelling were 100 per cent phonetic there would be for children no frustrating confusion among sounds and symbols. If the spelling were perfectly and consistently phonetic the child would easily make the connections between the letters and the sounds, with a minimum of help from the teacher.

It is precisely because so many *common* words are so flagrantly nonphonetic—like *through, bread, dough, said, one, was, two, eye, does,* and *says*—that the child will not automatically see his sight words as made of phonetic symbols. With these words the exceptions far outnumber the regularities—and they are high-frequency words in any English writing. They actually prevent a learning child from naturally perceiving that our spelling is consistently phonetic most of the time. These words seem to follow no reliable pattern and of course divert the child from realizing that most letters represent the same sounds on the vast majority of occasions.

By contrast, imagine the Italian child learning to read his language, in which every letter is scrupulously sounded.

Chicken "cacciatore" is pronounced with utmost fidelity. Both medial t's in "tutti" are lovingly caressed with the tongue. For the Italian child the connection between letter and sound comes very easily and might indeed come without phonic instruction. He could not watch his teacher saying words for a week without seeing it.

English spelling is so apparently irregular that most teachers don't know how regular it actually is. The long **a** sound is spelled eight ways—yes, and this is the worst—but they are eight consistent and regular ways that are used again and again, and the child can be made to recognize them if he is taught by easy stages. In fact most irregularities boil down to: 1) changed vowel sounds (largely short instead of long), and 2) silent consonants. The digraph *ch* is not dependable, but it has only three pronunciations—as in *chug*, as in Greek words like *chaos*, and as *sh* in *Chicago*. It is far better for a beginning child to know that *ch* stands for one of these three sounds than for him not to know that there *are* letters in words and that spelling is a method of representing sound.

Not all adults realize how much of a guide to meaning our spelling is. G. B. Shaw liked to point out that *fish* could be spelled "ghoti" [2]—yes, but it isn't. We have homonyms like *here, hear; pair, pare; there, their; gate, gait;* and there is good reason for having and keeping them. By spelling them differently we give ourselves an added help in telling what meaning is involved. As you go into it, it becomes a source of pleasure and interest to understand and use these facts. Henry David Thoreau spoke of the night noises, the baying of hounds and the crowing of cocks, as "evidences of nature's *sound* state," then proceeded to comment on his pun in these memorable words: "Such is the never failing accuracy and perfection of language; the chisel of a thousand years retouches it." What he meant was that it took a thousand years of linguistic development for the Latin word

[2] Ghoti: *gh* as in *cough; o* as in *women; ti* as in *position* or *partial.*

sonus meaning noise and the Old French word *son* meaning noise to become united with Old English *gesund* meaning healthy, into the same spelling and pronunciations in Modern English *sound,* while retaining their distinct meanings, and thus enabling him to make his pun. These qualities of the English language are a rich part of our cultural heritage. They can be preserved only when the language is studied with patience and devotion.

And now for an interesting sidelight. The Danes have adopted more recently than we modern methods of teaching reading, and their language is also somewhat unphonetic in spelling. The results of the newer type of instruction are summarized in an article:

> During the last 10 or 15 years all new primers have been constructed with a limited number of different words. All words used are very common words from the children's daily experiences. In spite of this work on more systematic and easy primers we find an increasing number of poor readers in the schools.[3]

And the author concludes that "the reading deficiency sometimes—perhaps very often—must have developed from certain functional abnormalities or blockings of the combining faculties or associative processes." The Danes are in for it.

Myth No. 4: Word-calling

One of the severe charges that the expert makes against the proponent of phonics is "Word-calling." Anyone who seems to be more interested in having a child sound out a word than tell what it means is accused of advocating word calling. A word-caller is a child who reads words, that is, pronounces them, without knowing their meanings.

In public discussion, we have been told of the little girl of nine who could read a whole book without under-

[3] Mogens Ellehammer, "The Reading Ability of Retarded Children," *Educational Forum,* March, 1955, pp. 295, 293.

standing a word of it, and of the Mongolian idiot who had been taught a little book word for word without understanding a sentence. But these examples tell nothing about phonic training: they merely show that a child cannot understand writing that he cannot understand. We propose to teach our beginners to read in books with ideas and vocabularies that are proper for their ages. If there were laborious word-callers fifty years ago (as we are continually told) it may well have been because too much of the material in, for example, the McGuffey Readers, was in the complex sentences and Latinized vocabulary of Victorian prose, which was simply too difficult for the average or slow child. But the fact that many children could understand those readers, added to the evidence of the complex style and vocabulary of their daily newspapers, should make us blush with shame today.

Again the truth is just the opposite of what the myth proposes. The word-callers we have seen—and there have been many—are people who have learned by look-and-say and are uncertain in their recognition of most words. They look twice to see whether they have got the word right. These people will stumble over words that they know perfectly well by ear, and not get much sense out of what they are "reading." Their trouble is that they do not know enough phonics and so cannot read easily and thus have no attention left over for the meaning. If they had been taught properly, word recognition would be so automatic that understanding would accompany it.

The child of very low I.Q. is a potential word-caller if he is taught by phonics, because his ability to sound out words will outstrip his ability to learn and retain word meanings. But if he is taught by look-and-say the strain on his memory will be still greater, he will not master more than a very small vocabulary, and he will end by reading with an even smaller vocabulary than he would have had with a phonic attack. The reasonableness of this truth is so evident as not to require elaborate proof.

Myth No. 5: Reading Readiness

Reading readiness is almost a body of doctrine by itself. A number of volumes and countless articles, to say nothing of many tests, bear their testimony to the importance of the concept. The theory is that children must not begin reading instruction until they have been through some preliminary training to ready them, perceptually and emotionally, for undertaking the task of learning to read, and until they have passed a battery of tests that measure this readiness. The preparation consists of the teacher's reading stories and rhymes to the children, having them handle books, training their perception of detail by having them look at a row of five words or configurations and tell which one is different from the rest, and developing a proper emotional set toward the task of reading. The tests measure such things as range of information, perception of relations, vocabulary opposites, memory span of ideas, and the ability to memorize a number of nonsense words by sight.

Now all this would not seem unreasonable, but there are some strange implications. In some schools much of the first-grade year is devoted to reading readiness, and during this time the child comes to learn that reading is a formidable task which he does not have to undertake until he is ready for it. The result has been that some children have decided they will wait a year or more before signifying their readiness. In other schools a half year is devoted to the program, and at the end of this time a segment—perhaps a half—of the children are started on their first sight words. It is seldom less than six weeks or two months before the "ready" children begin their first reading.

What is the "real" reason for the readiness program? It is that present methods of teaching reading are so slow and so largely unsuccessful that a reason has been found to justify deferring the attempt for a considerable period, for it is obvious that a child of seven will learn faster than a child of six. The program has the further advantage of giving official sanction to the notion that many children will have made no progress in reading during the first year, or even two. When the worried parent comes in to the school to ask why his boy hasn't learned any reading in a year or eighteen months, he is told that a battery of standardized and scientific tests show that the child is not ready to begin reading and that it would do him serious emotional harm to begin prematurely. We have heard of a number of parents who were given this answer for three years—after which they were notified by the principal that their child was doing very badly and should be given remedial reading.

Most interesting are the results of an extensive study in reading readiness, complete with scientific tests, begun in 1933, at the Horace Mann School in New York, carried through a number of years, published in 1937. These tests show quite definitely that there was very low correlation between early progress in reading and the abilities trained and tested in the reading-readiness program. Between intelligence, recognizing words as same or different, and repeating nonsense syllables, for example, and reading progress, the correlation was so low as to be insignificant; whereas the ability to give phonic combinations, name letters, write letters, and give letter sounds were at the top of the list and correlated *very highly* with reading achievement. Here is conclusive proof that the reading-readiness program does not prepare a child to learn to read; nor do the tests prove that the "ready" child will learn; whereas the same tests show that the child *who knows the alphabet,* can recognize letters, and knows some of their sounds is almost a sure-fire cinch to read fast and well. But reading readiness does not include teaching or knowing the alphabet.

Correlations of Children's Reading Achievement with Letter Tests and Other Measures [4]

Test or Measure	r
Giving phonic combinations	.84
Total letter score	.74
Recognizing words heard (really a letter test)	.74
Naming small letters	.74
Giving letter sounds	.70
Writing letters	.68
Writing words	.64
Naming capital letters	.63
Recognizing words seen (really a letter test)	.57
Mental age	.56
Matching total score	.45
Giving initial and final sounds	.45
Memory span	.44
Blending sounds	.41
Recognizing letter sounds	.39
Repeating nonsense syllables	.35
Chronological age	.35
Intelligence quotient	.34
Recognizing words as same or different ⎱ *	.20
Recognizing words as same or different ⎰	.17
Grip	—.04
Motor coordination	—.11

* Two different tests of the same kind.

The important point here is that the top items on the list—those which correlate most highly with progress in reading—are not on the reading-readiness test.

This table is to be sure not very clear as the reader cannot guess just what the tests included. Witty summarized this research with the comment that "Reading readiness is

[4] F. T. Wilson and A. Burke, "Reading Readiness in a Progressive School," *Teachers College Record*, XXXVIII (1937), pp. 565–580; reported in Paul Witty and David Kopel, *Reading and the Educative Process*, Ginn & Company, Boston, 1939, pp. 180–181.

in reality reading progress," and the observation that "Differences in reading progress can be explained mainly in terms of learning." [5] He concludes that none of the "traditional measures and tests of reading readiness ... is so satisfactory for predicting learning as is a measure of the child's present ability to name and sound the letters of the alphabet, singly and in combinations." [6] And yet this research seems not to have led to the teaching of phonics and the alphabet as a foundation for teaching reading. Ten years later another authority wrote that knowledge of the alphabet "seems to contribute very little, in many instances nothing whatever, to a pupil's proficiency in recognizing and reading words. In some instances, it is definitely misleading..." [7] Official universal theory and practice still ignore the alphabet and advise parents not to teach it to their preschool children.

We conclude this chapter with a note on a matter of language: The word *phonetics,* which means "the science of speech sounds," is an old and well-established word that is firmly defined in the dictionaries. The word *phonics,* which means "the representation of word sounds by letters," is too new to be clearly defined in the dictionaries, where it is not, generally, distinguished from the word "phonetics." *Phonics* is a new word because there was until recently no need for it: the fact that writing was a symbolization of sound was so obvious, so universally assumed, that no word was needed to convey the fact. Today we have got away from this basic and essential connection—and so we have a new word to enable us to say what should not have to be said.

[5] *Op. cit.,* p. 181.
[6] *Ibid.,* p. 182.
[7] Arthur I. Gates, *The Improvement of Reading,* third edition, The Macmillan Company, New York, 1949, p. 169.

Nine / Educationist Scholarship on Phonics and Reading

There is such a large quantity of literature describing research and experimental studies on reading that nobody reads it all. Most teachers in training of necessity read only the summaries or the quoted conclusions of such studies that they find in their textbooks, while the authors of texts and periodical articles quote the same "established findings" repeatedly until they have become hallowed by repetition. In this chapter we shall describe some of the studies that have been most influential in establishing and defending current practices, in order to display the caliber of research and logical analysis which is to be found virtually anywhere that one chooses to explore in this vast body of writing. And we shall also look at some typical passages from textbooks and the periodical literature.

Let us begin with one of the most important studies: the oft-quoted idea that learning phonics requires a mental age of seven and a half years can be traced back to a single study by Dolch and Bloomster.[1] These authors tested 105 first- and second-grade children on lists of uncommon one-syllable words and compared the results with their scores on intelligence tests. This was a test of phonic knowledge,

---

[1] E. W. Dolch and M. Bloomster, "Phonic Readiness," *Elementary School Journal*, XXXVIII (1937), pp. 201–205.

because these children had to sound out the words to identify them. Finding that the children whose mental ages were below seven (and some of those with higher mental ages) could do nothing on the test, whereas they did know some sight words, the authors concluded that greater mental maturity was needed to apply phonic principles than to recognize sight words, or that "phonic readiness comes at some time later than sight readiness." They add that these studies "do not tell, however, exactly when the teaching of phonics should be started. Ear training may begin earlier."

This study has been quoted widely as proof that phonics should be deferred until second and third grades, and has often been summarized thus: "Training in phonics before a mental age of seven years is wasteful." This statement is taken as gospel, and no one challenges it because "research" proves it, yet this is a sweeping generalization quite unsupported by the evidence.

The crucial question to ask of this study is, of course, how much phonics had been taught to the six-year-olds, and how had it been taught? And we find in the original study that the authors define phonics as "the use of generalizations about how letters are sounded, etc." In other words, the children had been taught a little phonics of the currently approved kind, but not enough to enable them to sound out any new word. The authors did *not* try teaching phonics by starting with letters and their sounds and progressing to phonograms and words as is done in the newer systems of reading instruction described in Chapter 10. All of these newer systems (as well as the older ones taught before 1920) actually teach phonics to children with mental ages of six or less, yet this fact is ignored.

The literature, further, reveals two diametrically opposite attitudes toward phonics. Whereas some experts say, "We do teach phonics," others still claim that phonics is useless and even harmful. For example, a very recent textbook says, "Although training in phonics has its uses, there is little evidence that it offers a cure for the ills of the retarded reader."[2] The authors of this text report as proof that Ewers, after studying 140 pupils in grades nine to twelve and comparing their scores on reading tests with their facility with vowels, consonants, initial-letter sounds, accent, and syllabification, found low or negative correlation between reading proficiencies and these skills. They then add the statement, "In our experience pupils taught by methods which emphasize phonics fail to look for meaning in the printed page." And they state in addition that "in one school system where phonics was stressed nonreaders could be found in every grade; some at the age of fourteen could not recognize the simplest words at preprimer level."

This latter statement is rather astonishing. Since a pupil properly trained in phonics could not fail to pronounce words on a printed page, it would seem that the school in question had an extraordinarily poor method of teaching phonics, and had in fact failed to teach it. Unfortunately, we were unable to investigate this school and see why the teaching failed to produce results. Most teachers in training and educationists read these statements, accept them as research findings and are convinced that phonics is, in some mysterious way, harmful, or at least useless.

A careful reading of the original study[3] proves interesting. Miss Ewers gave forty-three tests of "auditory discrimination" to 140 pupils. The pupils told which of two sounds was louder, which of two tones stronger, which note in a melody had been changed, which pair of complex sounds was higher or lower, also which syllables in words read were accented, and which of four words contained the diphthongs read. They judged words read as real or nonsense words, pronounced a word after it had been sounded out by syl-

[2] Maurice D. Woolf and Jeanne A. Woolf, *Remedial Reading*, McGraw-Hill Book Company, Inc., New York, 1957, p. 12.

[3] Ewers, Dorothea, "Relations between Auditory Abilities and Reading Abilities: A Problem in Psychometrics," *J. exp. Educ.*, vol. 18, March, 1950, pp. 239–263.

lables, and so on. Low positive correlations were found between scores on these forty-three tests and scores on reading tests.

On page 259 Ewers states, "What seems to be important in this experimental population is the degree to which the association between particular symbols and particular sounds has been established." This statement indicates that the knowledge of phonics correlates highly with reading ability, which is exactly opposite from the conclusion a reader would draw from the report of this study quoted above.

The statement that pupils taught phonics fail to look for meaning is another expression of the notion that there is a war between phonics and meaning. In one of the latest books we have seen, the author writes:

As we see it now, learning to spell words without knowing what they mean is a hollow and mechanical procedure—yet that is the way it was done for generations. Today our children build up a sight vocabulary first, so that spelling and writing will have some purpose.[4]

Notice the "logic" carried by that little syllogistic "so," implying that a child who recognizes that a printed word is a sound will thereby be prevented from grasping its meaning —whereas at the same time the statement is about spelling, not phonics.

The Reading Teacher, as its title indicates, is a periodical devoted to our problem; it is edited by outstanding figures in the field—Gray, Betts, Russell, Strang, and others. The December, 1955, number, edited by the distinguished Emmett A. Betts, is devoted exclusively to the phonics issue. And the Editor's Introduction solidly affirms the same "war":

We often work with children who can call words but who cannot read. That is, they have learned phonic skills but do not know how to *think* in a reading situation.[5]

[4] R. M. Goldenson, *Helping Your Child to Read Better,* Thomas Y. Crowell Company, New York, 1957, p. 85.
[5] P. 67.

We do not know where or how any considerable number of children in our schools today *can* "have learned phonic skills," because they are not properly or successfully taught; in effect, they are not taught. Where they are taught, as we shall show, the reading is impressively superior to the national norms. The proper learning of phonic skills cannot possibly interfere with a child's ability to "think in a reading situation."

Another article in this issue affirms that the average child is not "normally able" to "articulate effectively" the sounds of *sh, th, ch,* and *l* until he is six and a half years old, or of *s, z, r,* and *wh* until he is seven and a half years (page 85). These "facts" are offered as proof that the average child cannot be taught phonics until he is seven and a half years old. We affirm that a child of four can articulate these sounds effectively enough to make himself understood, and that a child of two or three can hear them well enough to understand many words in which they appear. We would also note that millions of English children have actually learned to read, well, and *by phonics,* at the age of five. It has not been, and we believe it cannot be demonstrated that these children were blessed with phenomenally advanced powers of articulation. Without "proof" on this point, we merely appeal to the reader's experience.

After a period when phonic instruction was almost completely discarded, most of the experts in the field of reading discovered that many children could not sound out familiar words and that inability to use a phonic attack was a characteristic of poor readers. Whereupon several of these experts worked out systems of phonic instruction and incorporated them in the teachers' handbooks that go with the series of readers which they edit. It is quite true, as the schools now say, that they do teach phonics; the question is whether these new systems enable phonics to be taught successfully. We think they do not, because they all defer the phonic instruction at least until the second grade, mix the teaching of phonic skills in with the various other methods of word attack we have described, and spread the phonic instruction, piecemeal, out through several years of primary schooling.

An excellent place to demonstrate how this evolution of phonic theory has led to difficulties and contradictions is the important text, *Teaching Children to Read,* by Adams, Grey, and Reese, 1949. Here we find a very earnest passage urging the teacher not to begin with letters and sounds and suggesting that she be prepared to dissuade parents from teaching their children the alphabet before they come to school:

> We are quite aware today that the child can actually read the long word "automobile" more quickly than the short word "opus." Obviously the child takes in the longer word with greater ease because he is more familiar with its meaning as well as with its general contour from having seen it on store windows, etc. If the child understands the idea, the length of a word doesn't matter when it comes to reading it.
>
> In spite of the objections to the alphabet method as a means of introducing children to beginning reading, not the least of which is its tendency to slow up the reading rate by forcing the child to practice the habit of piece-meal recognition, a number of parents even today, more than a hundred years after Horace Mann's contribution, ask why reading is not started with the ABC's. Faith in the efficacy of the alphabet method dies a slow death. Not long ago the principal of a school in a neighborhood that boasts many parents who are college graduates reported that 12 out of 50 parents, registering their children in the first grade last fall, proudly confided that they had taught their children the alphabet, so they'd be ready to start reading when they entered school!
>
> The wise teacher will therefore make provisions at the beginning of the first grade to help parents to understand the advantages of modern methods which do not make mastery of the alphabet basic in learning to read.[6]

[6] *Teaching Children to Read,* The Ronald Press Company, New York, p. 48.

It would have been scientific to test the twelve children who knew the alphabet and compare their reading progress, in six months or a year, with that of children who had not known their letters at starting. This procedure is not suggested. Nor, on second thought, would the findings have been significant, for knowing the alphabet *may* not help a child in a system where it is not used, although in our experience it generally does. Now elsewhere in this same book, these authors recognize with alarm the inability of poor readers to sound out words. They comment on the fact that poor readers cannot identify a word as a sound, cannot unlock a new word through its letters—and so they give a long list of phonetic rules for teachers to learn and transmit to their pupils in the third grade. Here are some samples from two pages of small print:

Developing Phonetic Understandings
  Silent: Consonants in words may be silent (*w* in *wren, wrong*...). Variability: Some consonants have variable sounds (*ch* in *Christmas* sounds like *k;* has another sound in *chocolate*).

Principles for Determining Vowel Sounds
  Position: If there is only one vowel in a word or syllable, that letter usually has the short sound unless it comes at the end of the word or syllable (*rent, cut, lot, gift; tip py, lad der*...).

  Silent vowels: If there are two vowels together in a word or syllable, usually the first vowel takes its long sound and the second is silent (*easy*). If there are two vowels in a word or syllable one of which is final *e,* usually the first vowel takes its long sound and the final e is silent (*blaze, disrobe, amuse*).[7]

These rules are a good summary of phonics, but they seem hard for a teacher to memorize, complicated indeed to teach to third graders, and obviously too difficult for first graders. It does not seem to occur to these authors that learning the letters and sounds is the first step in phonics that *can* be taught to first graders, because Horace Mann's "contribu-

[7] *Op. cit.,* pp. 352–353.

tion" (1838) is their authority for thinking otherwise. Faulty word recognition could have been prevented if the alphabet and sounds had been taught initially.

The phonic systems offered by the experts today are all of the same general nature. They teach phonics as a series of generalizations, as we have shown in Chapter 5, starting with the child's sight vocabulary, during his second and third year in school, if he is up to grade in his reading. And they teach phonics incidentally; that is, the children are helped individually by the teacher as they come upon words which they cannot read unaided. The reader who wishes to grapple closely with the officially approved method should try William S. Gray's *On Their Own in Reading,* Chicago, 1948. He sets forth "valid techniques for word perception that are in line with modern child psychology and modern ideas of reading instruction" and the "significant advances made in the teaching procedures used for developing word analysis skills." Here is a typical paragraph from this book:

With the unknown root word of more than one syllable, we consciously or unconsciously try to determine the syllabic units before we apply phonetic analysis when we try to determine where the syllables begin and end. In the word *nostril,* for example, the first syllable is *nos,* and the vowel in this syllable has the short sound (it is followed by a consonant); but in *notice* the first syllable is *no,* and the vowel has the long sound (it comes at the end of the syllable). The discussion of methods of identifying the sound of a syllable is given in the chapter on phonetic analysis, but we must remember that structural analysis is the first step in identifying the part of a word which constitutes a syllable—that is, a pronunciation unit.

The book contains 257 pages and gives a program for word analysis on five different levels, listing the skills to be taught children at the different stages of their reading development. It shows how to teach the child to use these phonic principles and "structural analysis" in connection with context clues, picture clues, and word-form clues. "A fourth-grader will find general form or contour especially helpful in discriminating between words that may be used more or less synonymously, such as *though* and *yet*." (Pray note the admission that a fourth-grader will not instantly recognize these words, whether by sound or sight!) "To this end, children at all levels should have abundant practice in noticing likenesses and differences in printed words. As they develop habits of careful visual scrutiny, the form of each word takes on a new quality based on their consciousness of the part or characteristic that distinguishes it from other words." [8] The complexity and laboriousness of these methods and of this prose are too obvious to require discussion.

Another volume that enjoys high status among books on reading is McCullough, Strang, and Traxler, *Problems in the Improvement of Reading,* (McGraw-Hill Book Company, Inc., New York, 1946). The central chapter of this work presents an interesting analysis of specific reading difficulties, with suggested cures. The authors first classify children as visual, auditory, and motor types, who should be taught to read by three appropriate methods. This means that the word or sight method is for the "visual" child; the auditory (phonic) method is for the "auditory" child; while the motor method, tracing words to learn them according to the procedures developed by Grace Fernald, is for the "motor" child. A child taught by the wrong method is apt to develop a reading problem. After describing the steps in modern reading instruction, the authors make a detailed analysis of problem readers, based on the observation that each type marks a stage in the learning process at which the individual has become permanently stuck. The descriptions may well be correct. There are six of these stages:

1. The child is born not knowing that reading goes from left to right. Failing to learn this fact, some read from right to left or back and forth at random.

[8] William S. Gray, *On Their Own in Reading,* Scott, Foresman and Company, Chicago, 1948, pp. 32–33; 46–47; 79.

2. The child is first taught words by their general shape or configuration. Some stop here and even as adults will confuse words of similar shape like *patter* and *yellow*.

3. The child is next taught to recognize initial letter sounds and guesses at the rest of the word from its context. The adult who has stuck at this stage may read *bent* for *bald*. Children at this stage are sometimes so intent on guessing the word that they ignore meaning or make random guesses when the material is beyond their comprehension.

4. Because the third stage works only for short, simple words, the child is next taught to notice endings and learns *s, ed, ing* and such "families" as *and, ill,* and *at*. People stuck at this stage will confuse words like *want* and *went*, in which the middle makes all the difference.

5. So the child is next taught to notice the middles of words. When this learning is imperfect he will, even as an adult, confuse *silver* and *sliver*.

6. The child finally learns a repertory of words and parts of words which he recognizes on sight and which he is supposed to use when he meets strange words, making them out without dissecting them into single letters. The adult who has not mastered this final step will be found laboring over phonetic parts or spelling words out in spite of the fact that he knows parts of them on sight when he sees them in isolation.

The variety of these problems, combined with the cumbersomeness of the methods that produce them, should be considered beside the fact that with the phonics system presented in our final chapter, Step 1 does not have to be taught; Steps 2, 3, 4, and 5 are never taught; and Step 6 is taught at the beginning, directly and often within the *first three or four hours* after the child knows the alphabet.

Having discussed the six stages of reading, our authors proceed to explain the weaknesses of a "phonic" approach—by which they mean sounding out a word letter by letter. Here is a sample:

In its attention to small units the analysis of the sound of a word may leave the amateur word sleuth with a lot of little parts, which he finds himself incapable of reassembling into meaningful wholes. In other words, this method requires the blending of isolated sounds to form the syllables it has broken—something like cutting oneself while trying to open a first-aid kit. The word "slake" can become a monster with "sluh" for a head and an "ake" on its back, if dealt with from a purely phonic standpoint; whereas if treated with a combination of phonic and visual analysis, it will become the easily sounded letter "s" with the familiar "lake" attached. This latter attack, heresy to the phonic diehards, is the sensible approach for the retarded reader whom the pure phonic method has left years behind himself in reading achievement.

What they mean by the "pure phonic method" is not explained. Alas, it is rarely used.

Here we have not one but three experienced teachers admitting unblushingly that our schools are turning out *adults* who confuse *patter* and *yellow, bent* and *bald, went* and *want, silver* and *sliver!* Yet this text has been used for years and apparently no one has questioned the methods used. No one has asked whether a child learning to read need be taught first to look at the beginnings of words, later at the endings, and still later at the middles of words. To anyone who has used the phonics approach in teaching reading, these passages are beautiful examples of unconscious humor.

As an example of the "pedaguese" in which some authors choose to clothe their views, we quote the interesting conclusions of a pamphlet on phonics:

Phonic training bears considerable positive relationship to oral skills of word pronunciation and word recognition.

Phonic ability is partially a function of training and, at the primary level, largely a function of mental age.

Training in phonics before a mental age of seven years is wasteful.

Formal phonic training at the early school level makes no measurable contribution to comprehension in silent reading.

At the upper elementary- and junior-high-school age phonic ability and reading comprehension seem positively related.

... Studies of maturation lead to the conclusion that phonic ability is an aspect of language facility and as such is inescapably related to organismic growth.

A final passage seems to say that children must be intensely satisfied with their reading before they can read:

These beginning cautions help to link symbols with their appropriate spoken words. Word analysis is out of place here. The immediate goal is one of idea and of intense satisfaction with a new process. Word recognition is only a remote goal at this time.[9]

Whereas some experts attack phonics and others introduce it piecemeal, a third group simply ignores it. *Why Pupils Fail in Reading,* by Helen Robinson, contains the research findings used as authority for the statement that failure in reading has multiple causes. Dr. Robinson worked with thirty children, aged six to thirteen, with I.Q.s ranging from 85 to 137, who had serious reading difficulties. Each child was examined and tested by a social worker, a psychiatrist, a neurologist, three opthalmologists, a speech-correction specialist, an otolaryngologist, an endocrinologist, a reading specialist, and the investigator, who acted as psychologist and reading technician. Many pages present the findings of these specialists, who tested and examined the children intermittently for five years and diagnosed their difficulties in group meetings.

The other specialists were apparently led by the neurologist, whose touchstone was "alexia." A child with alexia, he assumed, is *incapable* of learning to read. Now, *alexia* is in fact simply a word meaning inability to read. But this doctor apparently thought of it as a disease, like measles, or a hereditary defect. In general, if he found no neurological abnormali-

---

[9] Alvina Trout Burrows, "What About Phonics?" Bulletin No. 57 of the Association for Childhood Education International, Washington, 1951, p. 8.

ties in a retarded reader, he declared that he was a "true" case of alexia and concluded that the child *could* not learn to read. The diagnosis was disproved in several cases when Dr. Robinson subsequently taught the child to read. Where she failed, the diagnosis was "proved."

Most competent remedial-reading teachers and psychologists now avoid the term alexia, except for the case of the rare adult who has lost the power to read because of a brain injury or tumor; and most of them would deny that there is such a thing as a child with normal intelligence who is inherently incapable of learning to read. The cases are summarized in tables which display some of the most remarkable instances of reasoning in a circle that we have seen. Here are typical samples:

Anomalies Found by Individual Examiners	Factors Considered Important by the Group	Probable Cause
Case 20:		
Family maladjustment	Family maladjustment	Family maladjustment
Emotional maladjustment	Emotional maladjustment	Emotional maladjustment
Visual difficulty	Visual difficulty	Visual difficulty
Case 22:		
Alexia	Alexia	Hearing loss which may have been greater
Slight loss in auditory acuity	Lowered auditory acuity	Possibly a degree of alexia

And so on through the thirty cases, where the items in each column are approximately the same. The symptom is alexia. The important factor is alexia. The cause of the problem is alexia. One child, diagnosed as a case of inherited alexia, was given new glasses and better diet, but no remedial instruction—and he made little progress in reading. Anomalies found: alexia. Factors considered important: alexia. Probable cause: alexia.

The conclusion of this research (set up on the premise of multiple causes) is that a thorough study should be made of each child with a reading problem, that causes are many and varied, and that there was no single factor or cause that was consistently found in the cases examined. Although the author does not tell what methods she used in trying to teach children to read, we assume that she used the officially approved and recognized method, for her work was done under the direction of Professor William S. Gray (see pp. 114–115). No phonics test was given to these children and no mention of phonics is made in the text except in a review of the literature, where she states that poor auditory discrimination is frequent among poor readers and prevents the mastery of phonetics. Since these thirty children were selected because they could not read, they must all have been suffering from lack of phonic skills.

To go one step lower, we shall mention a piece of research often quoted, this time on reading readiness. The author made some careful measurements of six-and-one-half-year-old children and reached the conclusion that in order to have reading readiness a child should be 47 inches tall, weigh 47 pounds, have a mental age of six and one half, seven little bones in his wrist, and a 26-pound grip! It should be obvious at a glance that this author fell into just about every pitfall of error available to the unwary "researcher."

There exists a substantial body of excellent research by psychologists on maturation and learning. When a practical application, such as a method of teaching reading, is "based" on this research, it cannot be assumed that the method is "scientific" merely because the original research was sound. A scientist would devise a way of testing experimentally the actual results of the method in practice. He would never assume that he had produced an infallible system. Rudolf

Flesch in his search through the literature found eleven experimental studies in which a group of children taught phonics was compared with a control group not taught phonics. He reported that in each case the teaching of phonics produced better readers. In their attempts to defend themselves against Flesch's attacks the educationists have spread abroad the report that Flesch "distorted the research." An article by Dr. John B. Carroll of Harvard,[10] author of *The Study of Language,* is apparently the main source of this criticism. Of the many "answers to Flesch" which have been published, this is the only one that in our opinion merits serious consideration. Carroll read these same eleven articles and found four more that Flesch had missed.

In general, we disagree with Dr. Carroll's criticism. Dr. Carroll points out first "that it is misleading to draw the issue as between 'phonics' and 'no phonics,' and many of Flesch's distortions of research evidence stem from his failure to inform his readers precisely what kind of phonics instruction are involved in the research studies on which he reports." We find that the lack of discrimination between the different kinds of phonics taught and the failure to state precisely how much phonics the children were taught is inherent in the research studies themselves. Throughout his book Flesch *did* distinguish between systematic phonics and incidental phonics.

In every one of these articles, the *figures* show that a greater amount of phonics resulted in higher scores on achievement tests, although often by small amounts, it is true. Carroll, on the other hand, quotes the authors' conclusions, which, as in the case of the Dolch and Bloomster article referred to earlier, are not, in our opinion, always justified by the facts. These people are often emotionally biased against phonics and tend to find something which can be quoted as showing that phonics has bad effects. One author,

[10] "The Case of Dr. Flesch," *The American Psychologist,* Vol. XI., March, 1956.

after admitting that the phonic group in his experiment tested four and one half months ahead of its normal reading age (and therefore were 270 per cent better than the word method group, as Flesch points out), adds "Phonics should be used by the pupil as a tool and not as a subject matter to be mastered for its own sake." No one will disagree with this statement, but it is not evidence that phonics is harmful. In another study of first- and second-grade children, the group trained in phonics tested slightly higher than the control group, but the author concludes anyway that "it seems probable that much of the phonetic training now given should be deferred to the second or third grades." In trying to find a case against phonics some writers report that the phonically trained children read more slowly and less fluently than the word method children. This is quite possible with beginners. A tremendous amount of drill in books with a very limited vocabulary can produce some fast little readers in the early grades. The same children will be reading slowly and inaccurately later when they meet a larger vocabulary, while those who know phonics will have far outstripped them.

Carroll quotes another conclusion of one of the authors, namely, "that children who are given no phonics at all in the first grade do almost as well as those given gradual incidental phonics instruction, and usually better than those receiving conventional phonics instruction." There is no mystery here to one who knows the inside evidence. The children who receive incidental phonics in the first grade have probably learned the sounds of a few initial consonants and a digraph or two, such as *ch* and *ow*. This is a little help, but not much. Most of their training has still been by the word method. On the other hand, the "conventional" phonics instruction probably consisted of a good deal of drill on isolated phonic facts such as the "at," "ill," and "ate" families. This sort of drill will also be of little help since it gives the child a far from complete system of sounding out the words. Because of the little real difference in methods of instruction one would not expect great differences in results.

These studies are all by their very nature far from being carefully "controlled" in the scientific sense. It is quite certain that some of the children given no phonics had learned letters and sounds at home and therefore were able to teach themselves further phonics, while some of those who were taught certain phonic facts did not understand how to apply them to their reading.

Various authors of these studies claim that while phonically trained children do better in word recognition, the word method children do better on paragraph comprehension. It is hard to reconcile this statement with the statistics, which show that the former children test higher on tests of "paragraph meaning." These tests of paragraph meaning are always tests of comprehension.

The fifteen studies reviewed by Dr. Carroll seem a pitifully inadequate scientific basis for the reading program by which several million children are now being taught. We refer the reader again to Chapter 10. The reports on the Champaign, Hay-Wingo, Carden, and other studies are of large-scale, controlled, accurately reported studies of thousands of children over periods of years. They present overwhelming and irrefutable evidence that a reading program that starts with initial systematic instruction in phonics produces enormously better results than the currently approved method of look-and-say plus incidental phonics.

Like the other critics of Flesch, Carroll says that Flesch would have helped by "demonstrating ... some *tested* techniques in helping Johnny learn to read." Flesch did just that in his description of the Bloomfield method used in the Catholic schools and the Hay-Wingo method used in Bedford Park, Illinois, where he saw first-grade children reading fluently in third-grade books.

We have discussed Carroll's article at some length because we believe it had a great deal of influence in turning people against Flesch's thesis that our children are inadequately trained in phonics and in reading. Carroll is probably typical of a large group of friendly and intelligent people who assume that acknowledged authorities in the field of reading know their subject and should be trusted as we trust authorities in the field of medicine, law, etc. Dr. Carroll should take the trouble to inform himself about the alarming and increasing incidence of reading disability in this country, and then perhaps instead of advising parents to cooperate with the school authorities he will join a crusade to see that long-overdue reforms are instituted no matter whose feelings are hurt in the process.

Ten / Light through the Clouds

We are ready now to turn to a brighter side and deal with some comforting facts: (1) that reading is being taught easily and painlessly in various schools, and (2) that statistical evidence of the importance of phonics in the whole educational process is accumulating so rapidly that a drastic change for the better is now inevitable.

Evidence that the situation is so bad that change *must* come can be found in unexpected places. A recent survey of remedial reading, conducted in fourteen cities and villages in the New York and Philadelphia areas by a superintendent of schools, found 238 remedial-reading teachers, of whom 80 per cent had been employed within the past ten years.[1]

The author of this study visited the fourteen school systems to observe their programs and particularly to note what changes had been occurring in them. Whereas fifteen years ago he would have seen specialists working with elaborate diagnostic and training machines, he found rooms that looked "very much like a smartly dressed elementary-school library." The machines are seldom used now, even where they are owned, and the emphasis has shifted from diagnosis to the repetition of procedures employed in regular reading classes, although with smaller groups.

[1] C. D. Boney, "A Visit with Remedial Teachers," *Elementary English,* XXX (January, 1953), pp. 7–13.

The average remedial teacher has had "several courses in remedial reading." Whereas the university reading clinic has gathered a mass of data of which this author thinks it makes little use, the public schools do not use the special clinical procedures that accumulate such data. The program has been shifted from grade to grade, always with indifferent success. In one school, it was started in the seventh and eighth grades, later shifted to lower and lower grades, but was never satisfactory.

One superintendent of a small village with a highly privileged citizenry has tried a number of remedies for the reading problem because he is under constant pressure from the literate and responsible parents. He has tried special classes and reduced class sizes. But the reading deficiencies have remained constant, and he now considers restoring class sizes and abandoning the whole remedial program.

To conclude this story of failure and discouragement, the investigator asks whether outside pressures for better reading have not perhaps been excessive, whether the results have not been too meager to justify the expense, whether regression after any remedial program is not probable, and whether the work should not be deferred to high school, after the maturation of the student has improved his ability to learn. He concludes that the elementary-school program in underprivileged areas, particularly, should be "not so heavily loaded with reading." "Perhaps such a program will have many substandard readers," he concludes. "But it will have the advantage of at least attempting to teach children to do straight or balanced thinking, the lack of which many people believe to be our greatest problem. There are many who believe that this can be done even with a low level of reading ability."

It is the counsel of desperation to conclude that more straight thinking will be taught with less reading. This startling evidence shows that administrators in a large New York–Philadelphia area have given up hope of reclaiming

their retarded readers and are instead thinking about re-
ducing the amount of reading taught in their schools. When
reading and remedial reading have failed, they decide to
educate without reading! [2]

It is grimly amusing to note, in this connection, that a
current book on the reading problem contains a section,
with a list of suggested readings, designed "to help parents
through the difficult period of having a nonreader in the
family." [3]

These details of failure and frustration show, we believe,
that it will not be difficult to bring about a complete reorganization of reading instruction in this country. Superintendents particularly, we have observed, are more concerned for good public relations than for abstruse theory.
They have a pragmatic bent; when they are told of programs
that solve or avoid these troublesome problems, they will try
them.

Facts that have long been known to remedial teachers are
slowly coming to public attention by way of experiments
conducted in various parts of the country. The Hay-Wingo
program of phonic instruction is perhaps the oldest; it could
have shown the way out of our swamp many years ago, but
it has been scrupulously ignored in educationist writings.
Few people who have not read *Why Johnny Can't Read*
would suspect from the multitude of published attacks on it
that an extended description of the Hay-Wingo system in
practice, and of the brilliant results achieved by its use, in
Argo, Summit, and Bedford Park, Illinois, is the central part
of Flesch's book. A recent volume largely devoted to crush-
ing Flesch line-by-line does not mention it. [4]

The Hay-Wingo phonic approach unquestionably demon-
strates the waste of time and the unnecessarily high incidence of reading problems that go with the look-and-say

---

[2] See the conclusions presented by the administrator in Chap. 3, p. 29.
[3] Abraham, *A New Look at Reading*, p. 56.
[4] Duker and Nally, *The Truth about Your Child's Reading*.

method. It has been used with the same success with many other groups. One of the authors has used it successfully and has seen it used with striking success for several years. Yet we find no mention of it in the leading experts' books in the passages where they discuss the labored letter-by-letter "word-calling" that supposedly results from a phonic method of reading instruction.

What is this system? The Hay-Wingo text, *Reading with Phonics*, J. B. Lippincott Company, Philadelphia, 1948, charmingly illustrated, presents the vowels, then the consonants, then two-letter combinations to which a third consonant is added:

su	sun
so	sob
si	sit
se	set
sa	sat

It uses a combination of red and black lettering to set off the letter or syllable that is receiving immediate attention, and later it presents polysyllabic words with the syllables in alternating black and red. Having presented all the simple vowel-consonant combinations in easy words, it goes on to more difficult consonant combinations and then to irregular vowels, digraphs, and diphthongs—always with illustrations and a few sentences at the bottom of the page. At the back is a list of some 300 polysyllables (*cancellation, application, constitution, compensation, conversation,* etc.).

With this little book of 128 pages, and a reader, a child can be taught to read, easily, in a few months, so that he is "on his own" in any reading that is on the level of his vocabulary and understanding. Children taught by it have been consistently and impressively above the national reading norms. Visiting the first grade in Bedford Park in March, 1954, Mr. Flesch found the children able to read passages like the following at random from the newspaper:

Suburban Riverside's policemen were ordered yesterday to capture, dead or alive, a brown squirrel named Marge. The hunt means a great deal to the 10 year old girl who was bitten by the creature on Tuesday.

The first-grade class was divided into three groups. The poorest group was reading the Scott, Foresman reader for the first half of second grade; the middle group was half through the Scott, Foresman reader for the first half of the third grade; and the top group—which consisted of just over half the children in the class—was reading the Scott, Foresman reader for the second half of the third grade. Furthermore, the children did not read in a word-calling singsong. They read with expression, humor, and appreciation.

Results at Argo and Bedford Park are consistently a year above the national norm in all subjects, and there are no nonreaders except for occasional feeble-minded children. The high-school students qualify for an unusual number of scholarships to colleges and universities. The school spends five times as much on books as the average school system. And yet our own observation and experience indicate that these claims are low compared to what they might be if the initial gains of a good phonic teaching method were improved upon by continued appeals to the children's capacities with interesting and challenging materials of study.

One's first reaction to the Hay-Wingo text is that it might be a trifle cut-and-dried to take a group of children through the drill on letters and parts of words—even that it might arouse antagonism or bore a group of lively children; but we have used it and seen it used with such spectacular success that we know nothing could be further from the truth. Children are attracted by the book at once. We spoke to one young woman who was teaching for the first time and had been given a class of third-graders of whom a fourth were virtually nonreaders. Knowing almost nothing about her task, she had taken up Hay-Wingo more or less at random. "You see," she said, "I didn't know any phonics and I didn't know how to teach reading and I didn't know what to do till I found this book." She had graduated the year before from one of the country's outstanding schools of education, but her courses there had given her no clear-cut system that she could employ with assurance of definite results.

In her class now, everyone was reading (after four months) and making great strides in spelling, and the better pupils were reading independently for pleasure.

This young woman mentioned an experienced teacher, down the hall, who had just discovered Hay-Wingo and was using it for the first time with her second grade. The latter was likewise enthusiastic. Never had she achieved such results. The nonreaders who had constituted a fourth of her group (whom the first-grade teacher had reported as not having achieved reading readiness) had all quickly learned to read, including one child with an I.Q. of 75. Spelling was better than she had ever seen or dreamed possible in the second grade. The children were reading library books and newspapers. Parents of these children were already learning with delight that they were being spared their neighbors' worries about reading. When the town's reading supervisor learned of this success, she went right on talking about reading readiness to parent groups and denying that there were nonreaders in any of the schools. The teacher's spectacular success was ignored.

Hay-Wingo has been used with remedial-reading classes from the grades through high school. In one school there were children from eleven to eighteen years old who were reading below fifth-grade norms, many on second- and third-grade levels. They had all been subjected to interminable doses of "phonics" and had developed a stubborn and despairing resistance. They were shown the four-syllable words like *transportation* and *emergency* on page 122 of Hay-Wingo, which they could not read, and promised that if they went through the book one easy page at a time they would be able to read these big words by the time they got to page 122. Cooperation was secured at once. When these children were brought to concentrate on particular and definite tasks, so that they knew what they were supposed to be learning, they were uplifted with an enthusiasm that was touching to witness. Sloppy writing became neat. Lazy children became industrious. Particularly interesting was the way one boy who had been described by his teacher as incorrigibly lazy suddenly caught on to the nature of reading— "It just kinda dawned on me," he said—and was "transformed" in a few months into an "A" student. The whole group made an average of two years' reading improvement in just under four months. And they continued on up after that.

A courageous Superintendent of Schools in Sausalito, California, Mr. Marcus Davis, has converted all the schools in his town to the Hay-Wingo method. They use the book as standard for beginners and as a remedial text for problem readers and spellers through the eighth grade. The results have been so good, the children are reading so much more and so much better than they used to, that Mr. Davis tells a glowing story of happy children, happy teachers, and happy parents. His own pleasure in this accomplishment is tremendous. He began four years ago by appealing for volunteers among his teachers, to try the new system. Results sold themselves and now the system is used by everybody. A painless revolution has transformed both the school and its relations with the town.

Mr. Davis reports that there is a 50 per cent turnover among the children in the poorer section of town and that many of these children had previously been considered unteachable. Frequently their speech was so retarded it was hard to understand them. Yet they all learned to read and spell, and as a result of a year's drill in phonics they learned to speak clearly too.

Results on the Metropolitan Reading Test in one school were:

	Lowest Score	Median Score	Highest Score
1st Grade	1.8	2.5	3.5
2nd Grade	3.0	3.4	4.7
3rd Grade	4.1	4.6	7.5

The teachers of Sausalito were trained in a summer workshop led by a teacher whom Mr. Davis imported from Bedford Park, Illinois. Is there any reason why your superintendent could not do likewise?

A recent book by Romalda B. Spaulding, with Walter T. Spaulding, *The Writing Road to Reading* (Whiteside and William Morrow, New York, 1957), presents a tested phonics system that has been used with phenomenal success in the parochial schools of Hawaii for a number of years. Its introductory chapters (which we did not see until the present volume had been completed) touch on many of the critical points we have developed in detail.

Mrs. Spaulding reports that some classes have fifty or sixty children, yet no more than 5 per cent test below grade in reading, and about 70 per cent test a year or more above grade level. She tells of third-grade classes averaging 6.0 in spelling. The beginner starts by learning sounds and how to write, progresses to the spelling of lists of words and finally to reading. The statement is made that "for many children reading as such does not have to be taught." There is a most interesting description of the use of the system for remedial work with a class of high-school seniors.

An experiment at the McGill (public) School in New Castle, Pennsylvania, described in various articles by the principal, Glenn McCracken, uses colored "filmstrip" to dramatize the reading lessons. The bright pictures interest the children and elicit longer attention and better concentration. They move freely about the room, going to the screen

to point at words and objects, with results that have led
Mr. McCracken to challenge the concept of reading readiness—and with good reason.

For they have found at the McGill School that all their
children have reading readiness in abundance at the beginning of the first grade, and "Since 1949 more than 600 pupils have participated in this program and none has achieved
lower than average progress" [5] regardless of their scores on
reading-readiness tests and regardless of the considerably
more remarkable fact that some of the I.Q.s of these children
were as low as 80 (one was 71). All the pupils with I.Q.s of
90 or below scored low on the reading-readiness test (as they
always do, everywhere) and in a typical school would have
been declared not ready to begin reading. At McGill not one
of these children has failed to learn to read up to the national norm, and the averages at the end of first grade have
consistently surpassed the national norm by about half a
year, with many classes of children averaging higher than
the nation's norm for *third-graders*. One class, with a median
I.Q. of 106, achieved a median reading score (on the standard
Gates test) of 2.8 (i.e., eighth month of second grade) with
the best child reading at 3.4, by the end of the first grade.
This means that the class progress *averaged* as high as the
average national achievement of children nearly through the
second grade. In this class the *lowest* child scored 2.1, and
there were *no* children who failed to come up to the national
average. Even beginning teachers found that every child was
a good reader after one year. Children with I.Q.s between
70 and 90 could read any first-grade book with fluency and
comprehension.

No wonder Mr. McCracken concludes that "because we
have failed to provide reading programs with which we can
teach nearly every child to read, we have tried to justify our

[5] Glenn McCracken, "The New Castle Reading Experiment," *The
Reading Teacher*, IX, (April, 1956), p. 241.

predicament by over-emphasizing the readiness needs of the pupils"—i.e., placing the blame on the children.[6] It would appear from these results (which have been corroborated in a number of other schools) that the whole reading-readiness program could well be abandoned.

We have some questions about the McGill program, however. The reports show that, during the first years of the experiment, although every child learned to read, the correlation between reading progress and I.Q. was not as close as we should want or expect. For example, the charts show children with I.Q.s of 135 and 137 reading at 2.9 and 2.8 at the end of the first year, whereas such brilliant children (they are in the top 1 per cent of the population) could well be more than a bare year ahead of the national average. We note, further, that the acceleration of reading progress seems to slow down during the second and third years. No claim was made that the children were ahead in independent word attack. The best third-grade class described had an average score of 4.4 at the end of the year, which is not especially impressive. This may indicate that the look-and-say method with incidental phonics here runs into the usual troubles as the children get to the point where the burden on their memories increases.

The children of the McGill School come from middle- and lower-middle-class families, numbering many recent immigrants, and the classes seem to average a bit over 30 students. Intelligence norms are strictly average; these are not privileged groups. What has happened, apparently, is that the children have been led to concentrate and attend more than is possible under conventional methods. Because the whole class is taught at once, with no break-downs into little groups by interest or ability, there is considerably more total per-student time given to reading: instead of the pandemonium characteristic in schools where a large class is

[6] Glenn McCracken, "Have We Over-emphasized the Readiness Factor in Reading?" *Elementary English*, XXIX, (May, 1952), pp. 271–272.

broken up into several disorderly groups which cannot possibly be supervised by the teacher, all the children are paying attention to the projected slides of the day's lesson.

We wonder what will happen when Mr. McCracken and his teachers, having taken the bold step of abandoning the readiness program, take the second step and teach the alphabet and the fact that letters stand for sounds, *before* they begin work on the sight vocabulary. Being adventurous, they are sure to take this step sooner or later.

A third experiment comes from Bethesda, Maryland, where Lucille Schoolfield and Josephine B. Timberlake have been having extraordinary success, since 1944, with the Phonovisual Method, which they say "enables even a first-grade child, after mastering the consonants and vowels, to read and spell from 400 to 500 words without study." In eleven years at the Primary Day School, where the method is practiced and demonstrated, they have never had a non-reader, although they have made good readers of many children with whom other schools had failed previously.

We say "extraordinary success," although it is not really that; it is what ought to be happening in every school in the country. It should not be considered unusual for children to be able to read and spell from 400 to 500 words without study. If you will look at the list of the thousand most frequently occurring words in English in the Thorndike Wordbook, you will realize that they are words many three-year-olds know. In the *second* 500 words most frequently used, according to the Thorndike count, starting at random in the list you find: *sad, safe, salt, sand, sat, season, seat, seed, seek, seize, self, sell, separate, service, settle, seven, shade, shake, shape, sheep, shine, show, shop, shore.* The only tricky word there is *seize,* but an average six-year-old would know it and many others not on this list.

A trained observer, watching this system in practice recently, found that results were about the same in a private day school as in a crowded old school in a depressed area.

In both he saw eager six-year-olds playing tricks on and with words. "At teacher's request they would write the change that made *feet* say *feed*, and then make *feed* say *seed*. They were thinking up their own tricks, too." In the second grade of the depressed area school, he saw Phonovisual veterans trying to stump each other with big words like *educational, department,* and *recommendations,* which they had brought to school and written on the board. These classes use adult vocabularies, read serious and interesting material, and seem to have an unusual degree of poise and self-confidence.[7]

The system emphasizes quick recognition of words, the development of a sight vocabulary, and fluency and ease in reading; it develops these qualities because from the first day of school "sounds are anchored to letters." Between the two schools there was no "meaningful difference" in achievement. Both show results that are "unbelievably high" and absolutely valid statistically.[8] Here there is no nonsense about reading readiness or giving children from depressed homes "experiences" so that they will have something to read about. They just begin with letters and sounds, move very quickly into developing sight vocabularies, produce *no* reading problems, and surpass the national norm by many points.

The Phonovisual people have developed a simple spelling test of twenty words, with which they can diagnose any child's phonic ability. The twenty words use all the letters in various combinations (*shape, teeth, while, zone, cute, sprang, swept, quick,* etc.); when the Chicago *Tribune* offered, during the summer of 1955, to "analyze" anyone's child free, they were flooded with thousands of spelling papers that had been administered by anxious parents. The results were appalling. The Phonovisual people say that any child in the high second grade should be able to spell all

[7] *CBE Bulletin,* No. 5, December, 1956.
[8] Information about the Phonovisual Method may be had from Mrs. Marie Buckley, Principal, Primary Day School, 7300 River Road, Bethesda, Maryland.

twenty words easily. A retired teacher of thirty years' experience wrote in that the test was absurdly easy for any child
of fourth grade or above—too easy to prove anything. She
said that in the rural school where she taught, the test could
have been taken near the end of the first grade and passed.
Yet a young contemporary teacher from another community
wrote that the test was so hard as to be unfair. And a "dis-
maying number" failed to spell a single one of the twenty
words correctly! Many other children spelled twenty words
correctly, but many of the words they wrote down were not
the words on the test. There were third-graders with high
I.Q.s who could not read any of the words, fourth-graders
who missed nineteen and in repeating the test did not spell
a single word the same way twice. A child who had been
graded "excellent" in reading and received all "S" for "satisfactory" in spelling put down *cat* for the word *shape*. Children with I.Q.s over 130, in fourth grade, missed fifteen and
more of the twenty words. The 5,000 papers examined by
the Phonovisual people revealed phonic inadequacies which,
they said, could have been prevented without exception and
could even then have been eliminated with a few weeks of
concentrated phonic study.[9]

If the picture of Midwestern reading is frightening, the
reader may take comfort in the knowledge that a workable
system has proved itself beyond a shadow of doubt over
more than eleven years, without having a nonreader or a non-
speller. The method could easily be extended through the
country. It would save billions of dollars worth of human
resources that are now being wasted.

Twelve years of observation have confirmed Miss Schoolfield and Miss Timberlake in their conviction that reading
failure in the first three years causes emotional disturbances
that make learning to read increasingly difficult as time
passes. They mention this fact repeatedly in their literature,
and we cite it as confirmation of our own beliefs on the mat-

[9] See the Chicago *Tribune*, May 29, 30; June 14, and July 6, 1955.

ter. Their own pupils, who are making such unusual progress during their first year, impress visitors by their poise, assurance, and confidence in their abilities.

Extensive and impressive evidence of this sort comes from Champaign, Illinois, where a team composed of two professors [10] and Champaign public-school teachers has been working for several years with a large-scale, controlled experiment. Since 1952 they have been conducting an extensive program of phonic teaching, balanced by control groups of children, with comparable abilities and backgrounds, who are taught by the word method.

In their brochure entitled *The Champaign Story*, Urbana, 1955, they describe the word method of current practice clearly and simply:

> The word-memory plan begins with the whole sentence. Then it breaks the sentence down into phrases and words. This approach emphasizes word identification by memorizing words and by using pictures and context clues. Instruction in phonics is delayed until after the memorization of a basic sight vocabulary and is begun with the presentation of initial consonant sounds and some blends. (p. 1.)

Champaign had good schools; classes always averaged above the norm on reading tests, but its teachers were conscientious enough not to be satisfied because they knew that some of their intelligent students were not reading nearly as well as their abilities indicated they should; further, the percentage of students who fell below the national norm in reading increased as the years passed, and the scores on comprehension tests were always better than the scores on vocabulary tests. Even students who knew the sounds of all the letters, they found, were not using this knowledge to unlock new words.

So they undertook a revolutionary new program—"the

[10] Dr. J. Thomas Hasting, Department of Education, University of Illinois, and Dr. Theodore L. Harris, Department of Education, University of Wisconsin.

new phonetic approach"—which starts with the "presentation of the long and short sounds of the vowels," then the consonants, beginning what they call word analysis "before a sight vocabulary has been built."

Results of three years of the program show the experimental group (numbering in the hundreds of students) well beyond the control group that was taught by the regular sight method. At the end of the third grade nearly 75 per cent of the experimental group as measured by the Metropolitan Test were above the norm of 3.9 and about 25 per cent were below it. In the control group about 52 per cent were above the norm, 48 per cent below it. At the same time, 12.6 per cent of the experimental group were reading at the sixth-grade level, as compared to 7.3 per cent of the control group. Comparable results were obtained on the Stanford Reading Test. The experimental group were also "far better spellers" and consistently ahead in incidental reading skills like use of the dictionary and alphabetization.

The report considers the deficiencies commonly said to be produced by a phonic approach and finds that in every instance the experimental group excelled. They were not word-callers. They made the transition to supplementary reading materials more easily. Most of them were reading "naturally" by the second grade. Parents were happy. Professional satisfaction was high. The experimental group read more, and read more fluently, and somewhere during the first, second, or third grade their phonic skills were developed to the point where they could read independently. It is to be expected that further gains will be made from the early fluency of these children's reading. They emphasize the fact that, after a period of sounding-out, the child suddenly finds himself reading new words without any conscious attention to sounding them out. He just looks at the word and says it.

Another established system flourishing today in a score or two of schools in Long Island, New Jersey, and New York State, producing results year after year that far surpass those of ordinary schools, its teachers so enthusiastic that they declare they would resign rather than use another method, is the Carden system.

Miss Mae Carden, who directed the Carden School in New York City for twelve years, has developed a complete language-arts program that extends from the first through the eighth grade. She begins the reading program with phonic training right in the first week (she ignores "reading readiness"), but she says that phonics is only the first element in the language-arts program. Her children are trained in speech and sentence rhythms, in identifying the key word of a sentence, in summarizing and outlining, in handling grammatical terms—in short, in speaking, writing, thinking, and reading. Grammar, says Miss Carden, is thought; it is the structure of communication and meaning, and it can be taught with the first steps in reading. Begun in first grade, it produces understanding of the sentence as form as well as what it means.

Her children are also trained in subtleties of intonation and enunciation that are in general today practiced only by the most cultivated speakers. They learn that *taught* is a longer word, spoken, than *taut;* that the word *way* is pronounced higher than *weigh;* that there is a shade of difference between *fir* and *fur;* that the vowel of *meet* is higher (tenser) than the vowel of *meat!* These beautiful subtleties are taught in the first grade. We saw children in second grade, in Morris Township, New Jersey, easily identify nouns and adjectives and verbs, aware of the nature and structure of the sentence, and pronouncing new words without help.

Miss Carden is concerned with mental discipline and with substantial subject matter. Her children read no rubbish. They are grounded in fable, myth, the Bible, Grimm's fairy tales, the classics, and the beginnings of world history —so that they begin reading in the materials which she believes come first in the training of a cultivated person. To

Miss Carden there are no "masses." She despises the word. Democracy to her means giving every child the experiences and the discriminations that make intellectual aristocrats.

She says that a bright child can be taught a thorough working knowledge of phonics and be reading independently in any material that interests him after four months of hour-daily lessons. The slower child is usually on his own at the end of the first grade. Schools using the system report:

1. Never any nonreaders.
2. No retarded readers.
3. Children with I.Q.s as low as 75 (lowest 2–3 per cent of the population) are regularly taught to read.

Thus with order, procedure, drill, discipline, standards, and quality, little minds are formed for living and thinking with dignity and grace. We have observed children taught by the Carden system and found them happy, eager, and self-confident. They knew what they were doing. A cardinal requirement in her method is that the beginning child be presented with tasks at which he will invariably succeed. One *definite* step at a time produces confidence and mastery, without frustration or confusion. There is continual challenge and stimulation without boredom, bewilderment, or failure. We suspect that nothing is more important—or more often neglected—in the learning procedure than care for the learner's mastery of each step in a process so that he does not become "lost" along the way. Any adult knows how his own eyes glaze over and his attention fails when a specialist, absorbed in expounding his specialty, omits essential information in his eagerness to make a point. The child can be lost in any learning process when the teacher fails to consider just what he must know to get from step to step. Once the attention falters, there is sure to be trouble.

Miss Carden is a genius. Her knowledge, her powers of analysis, her understanding of children, and—above all—

her abilities in coordinating and organizing a program are dazzling. She has devoted many years to developing and perfecting her method. She can work for twelve or fifteen hours without a pause. Her goal is perfection, and she has infinite patience. She will not allow her system to be published by a trade publisher because she insists on personally supervising its installation and training the teachers in any town that adopts it. She does not think it will be practiced correctly unless she is there to direct and advise and see that it is done exactly her way—and she is undoubtedly correct. The workbooks, spellers, and exercise books are all privately printed and distributed by her. The readers, on the other hand, are cheap reprints of classics for which she provides graded lists. If you go to Miss Carden, do not expect any mild half-way measures! [11]

We have seen the Carden system practiced in a Long Island community with such success as to bring tears of pride and rage—pride in the devotion and intelligence of a group of teachers, rage at the fact that their success goes studiedly unnoticed in an area where retarded readers are legion and remedial reading an industry.

In the public schools of Franklin Square, Long Island, the Carden system has been followed for more than a decade. The reading scores of the children in the early grades are phenomenally high. In section after section of first-graders, tested on the Stanford Achievement Test at the end of the first year, the lowest pupil of a group of 30 scored 1.9 or 2.1 —and top scores ranged up to 4.5, 5.3, and even 6.0. The median scores in these classes were always above 3.0. This means that the lowest pupils scored close to the national average; whereas the class averages were more than a year better than national norms. Spelling averages, by the way, were a year or more higher than the reading averages. Gains

[11] Miss Mae Carden may be reached at 619 South Maple Avenue, Glen Rock, New Jersey.

of the first year *increased* during the second and third. Beginning a full year ahead, some second-grade classes averaged two full years' reading progress by spring, with the highest children reading at ninth-grade levels!

These results prevail through four primary schools in Franklin Square. They have no nonreaders and no retarded readers, for their worst pupils are close to the national average. Their most serious problem is with children coming in from other school systems. We talked with Mr. Cecil Spencer, Superintendent, and Miss Dorothea Freyfogle, Reading Supervisor—two people whose devotion was matched by their intelligence and flexibility—and saw in them the ideal from which so many of our schools have strayed. Mr. Spencer is in charge of a large establishment, with some thousands of children and a large staff, but he takes time to discuss pedagogical problems and results. He is interested in test scores and reading books, and he seems to know the names and individual problems of dozens and dozens of children. The staff at Franklin Square are rightly proud and pleased with their accomplishments, but they are not satisfied with them! They have seen Miss Carden herself in action, and they say that she could have brought any of these superior classes a year or more beyond their current performances. They aspire to draw closer to these goals.

It should also be said that Franklin Square is not a privileged community, although it is decidedly not a slum area. Teachers are fairly well paid, but there is constant replacement because young girls continually marry and leave. Interviewing, employing, and then training these young teachers in the Carden system make regular and heavy demands on the time of Mr. Spencer and Miss Freyfogle. Yet Miss Freyfogle dreams about teaching a kindergarten group to read toward the end of their year. She finds that the children come to school to learn and that they are disappointed if they are allowed only to play.

Miss Freyfogle was kind enough to give us a record of the results on the Stanford Achievement Test [12] for all the children in first, second, and third grades for the spring of 1956. It should be remembered that in an "unselected population" about 23 per cent of the children will have I.Q.s below 90.

The figures show no nonreaders, a small fraction of the children testing at or below the grade norm, and a much larger group testing from a few months to four years above grade.

Out of 558 first-graders, those testing above-grade in reading numbered 466 or 84 per cent, in spelling 531 or 95 per cent, and on the battery median 506 or 91 per cent.

The same figures for 589 second-graders were: reading 536 or 91 per cent, spelling 568 or 99 per cent, and battery median 559 or 95 per cent.

For the 645 third-graders the figures were: reading 504 or 78 per cent, spelling 508 or 78 per cent, battery median 518 or 80 per cent.

Of 268 children entering ninth grade in one school, 216 tested ninth-grade or above. Seventy-three of them tested twelfth-grade or above. Fifty-one children or 19 per cent tested at the seventh- and eighth-grade level, and *only one child tested as low as the sixth grade.* Turn to page 16 and compare these figures with Witty's report that typically 48 per cent of high school freshmen score below the eighth-grade norms.

And now for a most significant new development, where the brightest light shines through the darkest clouds.

With all the controversy over phonics, it is amazing, if one stops to think about it, that no one has undertaken an extensive and systematic testing of phonic ability among the public at large. It is not hard, however, to see why this has

---

[12] The reading score given is the average score made up of word-meaning and paragraph-meaning tests. The battery-median score is the combined score of the language and arithmetic tests.

The first and second grades took the primary form, the third grades the elementary form.

not been done: educationists have not been able to believe that phonics might be a problem beyond primary school, whereas the well-trained and literate adult still cannot conceive that great numbers of intelligent children and adolescents might not be able to sound out a word.

But a phonics test [13] (to which we referred earlier) that can be administered to groups has finally been developed, with results that will prove definitive if the public learns about them and becomes genuinely aware of what they mean. The test has been devised by Dr. Grace Brown and Dr. Alice Cottrell. Dr. Brown teaches psychology, study-skills courses, and remedial English at San Francisco City College. Dr. Cottrell has taught English in three colleges and has worked in the Counseling and Guidance Center at Stanford University.

These people wished to find out the extent of disability in phonics and its relationship to reading comprehension. After some preliminary testing of high-school students by Dr. Brown, Dr. Cottrell used the test as a basis for her doctoral dissertation.

The subjects were 1,650 freshmen at Stanford University, a state college, and a junior college—one-third of the students selected at random.

The test has ninety questions, on each of which the subject is asked to identify a printed nonsense word (like *talg,* *brel-checks,* or *terkog*) after it has been pronounced by the examiner; or to match a rhyme; or to discover a real word that has been spelled in an unusual way (like *coleckshun,* *tawkt,* and *raphtur*). Also included are many of the most frequently used primer words, such as *after* and *about,* as well as some harder words like *adventurous.* The test, constructed from errors actually made by college students, includes all speech sounds as represented by their various spellings. Since it is designed to measure the simpler aspects

[13] *Stanford Diagnostic Phonics Survey: A Group Test of Phonic Ability,* Consulting Psychologists Press, 4047 El Camino Way, Palo Alto, California.

of phonics, only college students with real phonetic disability would have any trouble with it. A good reader, aged anywhere from eight to eighty, will easily score between 81 and a perfect 90. We have seen many children and adults do so, proving that they know the relation between the letters and the sounds of our language. It was found that a score below 81 indicates that a student will have some difficulty in reading and spelling, while a score below 70 shows a definite need for remedial work.

And now for the findings. At Stanford 23 per cent of the freshman scored below 81, at the state college 61 per cent, and at the junior college 71 per cent. (Unselected high-school students score like the junior-college group.) For the top 10 per cent of Stanford freshman, selected according to scores on the college-entrance examination, in a university where competition for entrance is very keen, the median score was 86 out of a possible 90. Of forty-two students in this group, nine made perfect scores and only four scored below 82. The lowest score was 76. For the lower 90 per cent of the freshman class, the median was 84; 388 students scored 61 to 90. For a group of fifty-one in remedial English the median was 75 with a range from 49 to 90. The student who scored 49 was having serious trouble with his school work. About 90 per cent of the class scored above 76.

Freshmen at the state college, which has far less severe admission standards than Stanford, were not clustered so tightly toward the top, and spread much further down to a low score of 28. The median score for the top 10 per cent (thirty-one students) selected again by scores on the entrance examination, was 83, for 229 students in the regular classes it was 79, with a range from 48 to 90, and for 241 remedial students it was 70 with a low score of 28. Thus the median for the remedial group, which constituted about half the class, was lower than that of all but a small handful of students at Stanford.

At the junior college, where admission standards do not

exclude any applicant with a high-school diploma, the results were formidable. The median for the top 25 per cent of the freshman class—103 students—was 81, with scores from 59 to 90; the next quarter of the class had scores from 49 to 90 with a median of 74. The remedial group, which constitutes the lower half of the whole class, had scores as high as 89 and a low one of 14 with a median of 59.

All of the students were given a test of silent-reading comprehension, and a high correlation (67 per cent) was found between the scores on this test and the phonics test.

In general the results showed that there were three groups of students as classified by their scores on the phonics test: those who are good in phonics and good in reading; those who are poor in phonics and poor in reading; and the third group who are good in phonics but still do not test high in reading comprehension for one reason or another (such as a low I.Q.); but there is *no* fourth group who are poor in phonics but good in reading. In other words, phonic ability is a necessary but not sufficient condition for good reading.

Scores below 81 indicate that students will have trouble at Stanford with any course that demands considerable reading. At Stanford, 30 per cent of the students who scored in the 70–80 range were in remedial English. Of those scoring below 70, 80 per cent were in remedial English. The junior-college scores show that three-quarters of their freshmen are very poor readers who will stumble over any mature prose, commonly guess at or skip words, and frequently be baffled when they come upon a new word. Those with the lower scores are practically illiterate. After twelve years in the public schools some of them reach college unable to read very elementary material with ease and precision. Some of them are still confusing the simplest primer words. The colleges simply have to arrange courses adapted to the reading ability of these students. And let it be said these people are not stupid; they are educational cripples produced by our schools. And they *can* learn to read if taught phonics.

These findings will undoubtedly be duplicated all over the country when the test is given extensively, as we are sure it will be when its value becomes known, for the test will enable a school to identify those who need phonics. It will show that over two-thirds of our population and a sizable percentage of our college students cannot read ordinary adult prose with satisfactory comprehension. It has been known for years that the bright student who gets poor grades in college very frequently is the one who does not read well. This is very often the explanation for the students who excel in mathematics and science but have difficulty with English, history, and language courses. Reading correlates so closely with general college performance that the phonics test is apparently almost as reliable as intelligence or achievement test scores for prognostications of college performance.

When the extent of this ignorance of phonics becomes widely known, there will be a mass rush for phonic training in this nation that will affect our entire educational system. The educationists have been saying, "We *do* teach phonics." *These tests show that about 70 per cent of the population has not learned the phonics that, properly taught, they could have learned in the first and second grades.* This may be grim news, but we welcome facts so definite and a test that can be administered to large enough segments of the population to prove the case once and for all.

Eleven / Phonics Unlimited—
Initial and Remedial

THE "BORN READER"—AND HOW HE GREW

The cardinal point in our thesis is that all good readers know phonics well. With this tool they can come to know thousands of words at a glance. Now, the essence of this phonic knowledge is that it *functions*—that one uses it as a tool or skill rather than knows it as a set of facts or rules. For if you have to stop and think about it, you are inhibited and slow. The knowledge of the principles is there, all right, for you can see it in action. An expert fencer, boxer, golfer, skier, or tennis player can tell you a great deal about the techniques he uses; but he does not stop to think before he applies them. His goal is to learn his style or technique so perfectly that he uses it without self-consciousness or analysis and certainly without taking conscious steps from rules to actions. Properly learned phonic skills function in the same manner except that they are easier to master, use, and forget. The athlete who neglects to think about style will deteriorate; the reader will not.

These notions can be illustrated if we look at some types of readers and consider how their phonic skills were learned and how they function. Perhaps we can anticipate the question of the good reader who says, "I learned to read without any prolonged training in phonics. Why is it necessary today?"

This is the story of how one mother produced a family of good readers, forty years ago. The mother had had practically no books to read in her childhood and so had bought books constantly after she grew up. There were bookcases in every room containing several thousand volumes, including most of the English classics in complete sets and all the best children's classics, of which each child had his own share. Reading was regarded as a pleasure to be indulged after the day's work was done, and the parents spent every evening reading. Never for a moment had they any doubt that the children would have the same attitude toward books that they did.

The old-fashioned method followed in this, as in most homes of educated people, until a generation or so ago, was to give a child a set of alphabet blocks when he was about two. He played with them and built things out of them. At first he disregarded the letters, but gradually he began to notice them as any child will notice detail. Eventually, he would ask some older person, "What's that?" and be told that was *A* or *D*. Perhaps the adult would indicate that the small *a* or the cursive *a* on the other faces of the same block were forms of the same letter, but the child started with the capitals, which are easily distinguished from each other. There is no danger of confusing *B* and *D* or *P* and *Q* in the capital letters.

The child was at the age where one of his main activities and one of his chief delights was learning the names of things. He liked to point to an object and ask, "What is that?" At that age the child seemed to have no trouble associating the name with the object, and he was absorbed in this game for many delightful hours. He learned the names of the letters just as he learned the names *table, chair, shoe,* and *cup.* Since he enjoyed this sort of thing so much, his mother said, "Show me *A*," or "Show me *B*." He was delighted to do so. Sometimes he took the initiative and said, with great satisfaction, "That's *X!*" In order to learn the names of the letters, of course he had to be able to distinguish between them, and this he readily did. It was all a game—it was fun.

This mother also read simple books to her child, holding him on her lap so that he could watch as she read. Eventually he observed that the letters on the blocks were on the pages of the book. He also got the idea that mother was somehow turning these letters into a story that told about the pictures in the book. One of the books was an alphabet book: that was standard in every nursery two generations ago. Mother read this over and over again to her child, and eventually he learned to say it to himself. With the blocks and the alphabet book he could not fail to observe that letters represented sounds. "*A* was an apple pie. *B* bit it. *C* cut it. . . ." Intoning this with delight, he learned to connect the name and the form of the letter with the sound that it makes. The sound of *B* is contained in the name of the letter *B*. It became fun to recite the alphabet and even to sing it to a simple tune. Having learned them so thoroughly, the child could not fail to notice the letters on signs and boxes.

Eventually he would get a pencil or a piece of chalk and begin copying. In the corner of the nursery there stood a small blackboard with the letters on a scroll over it. From time to time he practiced copying the letters on the blackboard until he was able to write all four *A*'s—large and small printed letters and large and small written letters. By the time he was four these letters had become a part of him—old friends that he never could forget.

In the meantime, of course, he was using language as communication in all his waking hours—talking, asking questions, conversing with others. At bedtime he demanded that something be read to him, and probably before he was four the idea that he would like to read himself had occurred to him. In imitation of the grown-ups he would recite a well-known story while looking at the book in which it was printed. Finally he learned to print his name and a few other words on his blackboard. At this point he had what the modern educationists call "reading readiness."

Finally, he took the initiative, found a primer, managed to get the attention of an older sister, and got her to tell him the first words in the book. And thus he started reading without realizing he was taking any special step. Someone simply pronounced the words in a book for him, and since the visual images on the page were absolutely clear and distinct—being made up of his old friends, the letters—he had no trouble making the connection between the printed and the spoken word and he realized how the letters represented the sounds. It was so much fun, such a pleasant game, that he went on to learn more words, for he saw that new words were made of various words and syllables with which he was already familiar. When he knew *boy, toy* said itself at a single glance.

The story itself was interesting, held his attention, and demanded to be finished. A few more steps in this process and he was reading independently—and it had all come about by easy and natural degrees, with no discipline, no "drill," no boredom, no confusion, no psychological tension.

One of the girls in this family, having "taught herself" to read, eventually went to school and of course wanted to come home and play school with the young brothers and sisters. She coaxed her father into buying three identical primers and proceeded to play school. The younger children, having gone through this "reading-readiness" stage, were delighted to cooperate in the reading lesson. But the class broke up in about two weeks because by that time the children were two-thirds through the primer and found that they could read on their own and get through the stories faster than their young teacher could lead them. Occasionally they needed help with a word, but they accumulated vocabulary rapidly and in a few months were able to read stories as difficult as those which they understood when they were read to them. Once launched into the field of books, of course, they constantly met words not in their speaking vocabularies. Occasionally they asked a meaning from an adult, but mostly they just figured them out for themselves from the context and thus continually enlarged their vocabularies without effort.

They frequently used these self-acquired words in conversation—occasionally with the accent misplaced so as to cause considerable mirth on the part of the grown-ups. The parents had an odd system of encouraging this habit of reading. They laid down the rule that children should not read in bed but should turn out the light and go to sleep. Children were not allowed to read in the morning before getting up because it was "bad for the eyes." Both rules were constantly disregarded. Reading came only after the dishes were dried,—or after the beds were made and the room cleaned up on Saturday morning. They were also told to go out and play in the sunshine instead of reading. These injunctions had the effect of making reading a reward and a pleasure, to be indulged in after duties had been performed.

On the rare occasions when neither parent was home for a meal and the children ate alone, they all brought books to the table, propped them up on milk pitchers and sugar bowls and read without speaking a word to each other.

As a matter of course they all eventually ran into books with difficult passages. One boy at ten was reading *The Three Musketeers*, for by that age he had exhausted the children's books in the house. He paused in his reading, said to an older sister, "Listen to this," read aloud a paragraph concerned with ecclesiastical politics, added, "I can't understand a single word it says—isn't that terrible?" and plunged back into the story. It was taken for granted in those days that *any* child could read anything so far as pronouncing the words was concerned. This doesn't mean he was a "word-caller," but that there were still some words he didn't know and some ideas (or sentences) that were too complicated for him.

This mother was actually using the most extreme progressive method in teaching her children how to read. She aroused interest, although unconscious of doing so, waiting until the children were ready to read, and did not require that they do anything in the line of reading that they did not want to do. The program was completely successful and achieved a result that looks dazzling by modern standards. All of the children became avid readers and found school work easy.

These children were examples of the really excellent readers to whom reading was so easy that there seemed to be no problem of learning. Nor were they unusually precocious; they did not start until they were five or six. We have known many children who started to read at three or four and some as early as two and one-half. Most of them learned without any prolonged course in phonics, but as far as we know every one of them knew the alphabet before he started, and was aware that letters "said" sounds. Once he started, he read fluently and easily with only an occasional mistake, with no period of guessing, miscalling words, or failing to get the meaning.

These lucky children seemed to the casual observer to learn with almost no instruction. As we have shown, however, they had had a thorough grounding in the names, shapes, and sounds of the letters which enabled them to learn, while doing their earliest reading, the basic phonograms of English. Soon new words were perceived as composed of familiar syllables which instantly said themselves to the child. They are *not* examples of children who were not taught phonics, but rather illustrations of the importance of phonics.

THE FORMALLY TRAINED READER

There are also among our older acquaintances a considerable number of people who were deliberately taught a more or less complete system of phonics and then started at once to read a fairly advanced book, skipping primers entirely. Half a dozen of them were taught by grandmothers or mothers and started by reading the Bible.

The best method of all is to take the child step by step through a complete system of phonics, teaching him, not rules, but all the phonograms (*as, at, ite, ine, ime,* etc.) of English and letting him start reading whenever he wants to. It can be done with this system in a few hours. This makes for faster progress and far better spelling.

It is hardly necessary after the studies we have quoted to defend a "synthetic" phonics system. Such a system is quickest for beginners, and, in our experience, the best way to break up bad habits in older ones. It attacks the whole problem from a new angle so that the remedial student can come back to reading later with new and improved habits and fresh courage.

With all the phonics systems on the market, some of which are good, some bad, it is necessary to offer an explanation for producing another one. It is simply that after extensive experience with other systems, we find that this one proves to be faster and more direct.

We skip prolonged analysis of oral words into their component sounds and the learning of the short vowel sounds in isolation, which are difficult to teach. After all, most adults could not give the sound of short *u* upon demand. But we do teach the vowel sounds in combination with consonants more quickly than other systems do. Practically no rules are required, since we find that most literate adults who are not professional teachers know no rules. Instead we proceed at once to the phonograms that make up English words, arranged so that learning them is easy. The next step is to show the student that he can read one-syllable words at sight without "sounding out." At the end of a few hours he finds himself reading long words in the same way. The system results not in "sounding out" or "attacking" or "analyzing" or breaking up into syllables, but in instant recognition. The basic process is to form an association between the sounds of the spoken word and the letters representing the sounds and then to connect these two with the meaning. It is the meaning which makes the word a whole, and an easily remembered whole.

The system differs from some others in that it is not limited to regularly spelled words. We show that the so-called nonphonetic words also follow regular patterns.

It has been used for twenty years on beginners of five and a half and middle-aged adults, retarded second-graders and college graduates. Since it covers the whole of phonics, it will discover the weak spots of every student. It is surprising that the second-graders and the college graduates who have had a history of trouble in reading and spelling make the same mistakes and stumble at the same places. It is short enough to be used as a test yet contains enough drill for a cure, and can actually be *taught* in less time than is taken to administer the elaborate diagnostic tests of some of the clinics.

TEACHING YOUR OWN CHILD

There are two pitfalls in teaching your own child. As a parent you may not have had the experience and training to know how to go about it. You perhaps lack self-confidence and your offspring may be very doubtful of your ability. School people in general give the impression that they would as soon toss a child to hungry lions as turn his education over to mere parents. The answer is that if you will use a book written by an experienced teacher and follow the recipe exactly you will do very well.

The Calvert School of Baltimore has for years taught children all over the world by correspondence. Army, Navy, missionary, diplomats' wives in foreign countries have taught their children successfully. You can too. The authors' friends have repeatedly helped their own children with great success.

The parent's other pitfall is impatience, which can be avoided by the same procedure of following a book. Few adults realize how difficult the beginning steps in a subject can be for a child, or just what these steps are. What seems obvious to him may be pure Greek to the young one.

One story will illustrate what we mean. A six-year-old girl of our acquaintance started school, after a summer in which she could hardly wait for the glorious moment when she would be taught to read. She came home the first day depressed because she had learned only three words, *red, yellow,* and *green.* Then, being a happy and resourceful little girl, she added, "But I am teaching myself to spell *red.* The first letter is *r* and the next letter is *e* and tomorrow I am going to teach myself the rest of it." Why, asks the adult, did she need two days to learn three letters? Why didn't she simply look at the word and say *r-e-d?* After two weeks of reading-readiness activities this little girl decided that reading could wait no longer, found a book, got her mother to "tell her the words" for two weeks, and thereafter read on her own with only occasional help. And yet it took two days to learn to spell *red.* Think of this if you are tempted to become impatient.

Teaching a Beginner

When you are teaching a beginner or a child who has learned a few sight words in the first grade, the problem is simple, as we showed in our description of the family of good readers. You start by teaching the names and appearances of the letters of the alphabet, which you may want to print on cards; or you may use blocks. Start with only one letter the first day. When the child has mastered it, he will be interested in going on to other letters. Start with the capitals, because they are easily distinguished from each other; and be sure that the child can print every one of them, for you will not be sure that he knows them unless he can print them.

Lower-case letters should come second. Make a game of it, and your child will be asking for more each day. Let him take the initiative wherever possible. He will soon be noticing letters on signs and cereal boxes. While the names and appearances of the letters are being mastered, casually introduce the idea that each letter "says" a sound and that these sounds occur and recur in our words. Show him that our words are made up of sounds and that these letters are ways of writing these sounds. When he has learned that *b* says *buh,* you can show him that *ball* starts with that sound and you can print the word for him to look at. As he progresses in learning the sounds, he will take the initiative in trying to decipher an occasional word in a sign or a newspaper. When he has mastered these first steps you can start on the phonic system, explaining that it will show him how we read.

While you are teaching it, and probably long before you reach the end of it, your child will demand that he be allowed to read something. By all means let him start at once. And now for an important point. You do not have to make him sound out every word; just tell him the words one at a time while he looks at them, and then explain "*c* says *cuh* and *a* says *ă* and *t* says *tuh,* so you can see it says *cat* and it couldn't say anything else but *cat.*" He will be delighted to read the sentence after you and then will recognize the same word in the following sentences. You may possibly want to print some of these first words on cards and play games with them so that they become firmly fixed in his memory, though this is frequently unnecessary. Remember, incidentally, that these "lessons" may be only two or three minutes long and that ten minutes makes an ample lesson at the start. When your child expresses an interest, you always follow his initiative; but you will of course return to the phonic system and work on it, whenever opportunity occurs, until you have completed it through page 254. Make every association with reading pleasant. Praise every step and every accomplishment; don't press; don't criticize; don't allow failure. When the child pauses, you supply the syllable or word immediately; don't leave him floundering; but if he says, "Don't tell me," obey him. Don't worry; above all, don't hurry.

Remedial Teaching

The student who has tried to learn to read and failed is discouraged and embarrassed. He may have given up, or he may be trying too hard with the wrong method and finding that the harder he tries the worse he gets, for he does not know where the trouble centers and therefore cannot be expected to help himself. He needs to be shown how to bring his attention to bear on precisely the right things in the right order. Remedial reading is not a problem in motivation or effort or interest, but rather of getting the right skills functioning easily and naturally. This is accomplished not by struggling along on the level where he is now failing, but by going back to the very beginning, starting all over again, and teaching the things he missed. Only thus will his confusions be cleared up. The phonics system is designed to do precisely that. It gives the elements of phonics step by step in such a way that they are learned as skills rather than as rules.

Since your remedial reader is afraid of failure, however much he may try to hide the fact, take every precaution to avoid embarrassing him further. It may even be inadvisable to ask him to read to you or to give him a test. You probably have a pretty fair idea of what his difficulties are anyway.

Getting the cooperation of a first-, second-, or third-grader is generally easy enough, but the adolescent will often resist your attempts to help him, and adults are nearly always difficult to get hold of. They learn rapidly if they will cooperate, but the trick is to get them to the point where they are willing to start. These people are apt suddenly to discover that they are busy elsewhere and have no time to learn. Their resistance may be due to several causes. They had phonics and it did not work; they are embarrassed at having to go back to first-grade work; some of them cannot face the fact that the whole explanation behind years of misery was something so simple that it could have been taught in a few hours; and some of them have learned to live without reading and just do not want to bother. In practice we find that if you can persuade your student to try the first few pages of the material, there will be no further trouble in getting his cooperation because he will see its value at once. Underneath he is really desperately eager to learn to read and spell, and once he is convinced that this is possible, there will be no trouble in getting him to work at it. He needs to relax in order to learn, but you cannot get him to relax by commanding him to do so; nor will he believe you if you say, "Of course you can learn to read."

A method that has succeeded many times is to explain that millions of Americans have had trouble with reading, that a different method of instruction is now being used in many parts of the country, and that we should like to show him how he would have been taught to read if the proper method had been followed. "Here is some material that has been used for twenty years with people of all ages. It explains the system by which our words are written down. It is all here in a few pages, and you can learn it in a few hours. Once you have gone through this material you can teach yourself to read. All I ask you to do is to pretend that

you are six years old and cannot read a word; I will show
you how you should have been taught. Instead of doing
a lot of talking, let's just begin, shall we?" This demand is
so simple and this way of putting it makes it so evident he
is not going to be asked to do anything impossible that he
can forget his fears and relax, and you will find him ready
to cooperate.

There is one group of retarded readers who seem to
suffer not from too little phonics but too much. They sound
out every letter of every word and then try to put the sounds
together and thus manage to limp along at a rate of fifteen
words a minute. Upon investigation, it turns out that no one
bothered to tell them the basic facts. In reading the word
"play" they will make a sound for *p*, one for *l*, another for
a, and a last one for *y*, and then proceed with the help of
the context to try to figure out the word. They have not been
taught the sound of *pl* as a unit or that the two letters *ay*
have a single sound. These children are really not examples
of too much phonics but of too little, badly taught, and they
will profit by starting with the phonics system too.

The most interesting people of all to work with have been
the adults, some of them college graduates, some with advanced degrees, many of them extraordinarily intelligent
and able people. They have had varying degrees of difficulty. Some read slowly, skip words, and spell badly; others
have learned to avoid either activity and rely on wives and
secretaries. Once they have got into the phonics work far
enough to feel that they understand the system, they open
up and discuss their troubles. They tell you they did not
know words were sounded from left to right, that they have
to look at a word twice to be sure they have it right, that
they always saw words made up of hills and valleys (the
consonants and vowels) and they just gave up on the valleys.
One student had never had an inkling that there was any
connection between sounds and letters. One had learned
the international phonetic alphabet but had never realized

it could be applied to anything. Several had had French phonics and still lacked the basic idea that there is such a thing as an English phonic system. Some have learned over the years with heroic effort to read and spell ordinary words as sight words, but never noticed that *c* has two sounds. Some can't read a four-letter nonsense syllable. They read *employ, employment,* and *employee,* but when presented with *ploy,* read it *polly.*

Progress with an intelligent adult may be unbelievably rapid, for while you are teaching phonics you are actually accomplishing a version of psychotherapy. Taking an adult through the phonics material, you are the analyst taking his patient back through his past, bringing up the sources of his fears and anxieties and helping him free himself from these crippling emotions as their causes are understood. Through the phonics exercises you encounter one by one all the problems and incidents that confounded him and produced his "complexes." As he masters these situations, his fears drop away and a real personality change may take place. He discovers that he is no different from other people, that he merely got off to a bad start.

Besides the work in phonics, another valuable way to help a badly inhibited child is Fernald's method of tracing. If, for instance, the child you are working with is a third-grader who can't read, can't write the letters correctly, and can't spell, this may be invaluable. He has probably been getting zero on his spelling lessons. It is unfair that he has to fail the spelling test every Friday, but there is no chance of his learning enough phonics this week to master the spelling of fifteen words he cannot even read. Therefore, write the words of his spelling out for him with black crayon in letters an inch high, underline the separate syllables and have him trace over the letters with his fingers while pronouncing the syllables until he can write the word from memory. Be sure he says the syllables and not the letters as he writes. Thus he will form an association between the letters and the sounds of the words. If he traces his lesson each day during the week, he will have all the words by Friday, and an "A" on his spelling paper will give an enormous boost to his self-confidence. Later he will be able to learn his spelling by reading the words over once, but he may need to trace for a month or so. The tracing results automatically in vastly improved handwriting.

One bright, hard-working little boy was found to have developed his own method of teaching himself his spelling lesson. As he printed the word "much" he chanted, "One hump and another hump, an upside-down hump and a sideways hump, a line and another hump"; but alas, on the test he got the humps mixed. As this boy started phonics he also traced his spelling words. The work on spelling, of course, in turn helped his reading. Eventually he found he could master a whole list of spelling words just by reading it once.

After the work on phonics, then what?

The school people say that "reading is more than phonics." Of course it is! The next step is to read connected prose, getting the meaning not only of separate words but of the whole selection. Some children make this step by themselves, but most need a period of practice and should be encouraged to read a book out loud. It is not possible to give exact rules for this step except to say that if you will follow your natural impulses you will do very well. The authors' friends have proved to be exceptionally good teachers of their own children. In general, your role is to be an interested, patient, and invariably courteous audience.

Since the student should finish the phonics work confident that he can read any word he comes to, he will be relaxed and eager to start. Help to direct his attention to the story by comments about it and by getting him to discuss it with you. If he has been accustomed to reading inattentively, ask him questions about what he has just read or pose a question and have him read to find the answer.

Because going through the phonics system takes only a

few hours, there is not time for much growth in reading to have taken place. Assume that your student ends the system on the same level of ability with which he started, and start out from there. If he was reading a primer, get something a little bit harder than the primer. If he was reading a college textbook in chemistry, help him with the next chapter. He is ready now to take rapid strides in reading, and he just needs some practice. It is impossible to give a list of suitable books for everybody from a five-year-old to a college graduate, but here are some suggestions.

The first reading matter for a child who has been a complete nonreader may well be a story or article about his hobby dictated by him and typed by his teacher, who may then write another selection, using the same vocabulary, and have him read that. The same nonreader will be helped by reading a book which someone has first read to him.

Avoid the current primers which are very bad, not just because they are dull but because the text literally does not make sense; the meaning is in the pictures, and the sentences are composed almost entirely of abstract words such as *was, is, look, see,* and a few proper names. These little words are the hardest of all words to learn, since a little child has probably never thought of them as having any individual existence. They should be learned among concrete words and interesting subject matter.

A good first reader is *Straight Up,* by Henry B. Lent (The Macmillan Company, New York) a story about a boy and a helicopter. There is also a sequel called *Straight Down.* The Walt Disney series of school readers is also popular. On the other hand, the child may prefer to work on the next story in his school reader in order to show the class he has learned to read. Encourage the child to sound out words for himself, but do not hesitate to help him if he asks for help.

Really sure-fire hits for people of almost any age are *Curious George, Curious George Takes a Job, Curious George*

Rides a Bicycle, and *Curious George Gets a Medal,* by H. A. Rey (Houghton Mifflin Company, Boston), about a monkey who gets into funny predicaments. The illustrations are delightfully funny and appeal to almost everyone. *Curious George* should have a gold medal for the number of children it has convinced that reading is worth the trouble. The stories are short but the vocabulary includes occasional long words like *fascinated* that are calculated to gratify the ego of the learner.

Little girls particularly like Clarence Anderson's books, *Billy and Blaze* and *Blaze and the Gypsies* (The Macmillan Company), and boys will enjoy them too. The famous Dr. Seuss books are very popular with most children, and he has written one, *The Cat in the Hat* (Houghton Mifflin Company), which can be read by anyone with a first-grade vocabulary.

Good books for more advanced readers, those able to read at a third- or fourth-grade level, are the *Childhood of Famous Americans Series* (The Bobbs-Merrill Company) and the *American Adventure Series* edited by Emmett A. Betts (Franklin Watts, Inc.). For boys interested in science there is a series of books by Herbert S. Zim (William Morrow and Company) and the *All About Series* by various authors (Random House, Inc.). *The Wizard of Oz* is remarkably good for remedial reading. It looks big and difficult and quite unlike the school readers, yet has a fairly simple vocabulary, and once the child has been helped through the first two or three chapters he will find he knows the words and can go on with no difficulty.

Any children's librarian will be glad to suggest the most popular books which most children love, such as Ruth Ganett's *My Father's Dragon* and *Elmer and the Dragon* (Random House, Inc.), Phil Stong's *Honk the Moose* (Dodd, Mead), Pamela Travers' *Mary Poppins* (Harcourt, Brace), etc. You will just have to look them over and judge for yourself which ones to try out and find out which appeals. The limericks in *The Singing World* by Louis Untermeyer (Harcourt, Brace) (page 281 on) which make fun of English spelling are entertaining and encourage an interest in words.

For boys of twelve or fourteen who are just starting in to read, try *Andy and the Lion* by Daugherty (The Viking Press, Inc., New York). It has a very little simple text and lots of amusing pictures and still does not seem too childish. From there go on to short selections, such as headlines in the newspaper, the captions under pictures in *Life*, or books of cartoons. Humor is the thing to look for unless your child is scientifically minded, in which case he may want to read about the atom or engines. If he prefers sports, he will probably enjoy short selections from the sporting page of the newspaper more than a written-down book about baseball. In general try to find something that looks grown up, which will give your student the satisfaction of getting out of the baby class. Selected articles from the *Reader's Digest* are excellent.

Once reading is well under way, do read good books, classics by great writers. Read Kipling's story of Rikki-Tikki and his "Ballad of East and West," the Twenty-third Psalm, the poems of Emily Dickinson, something you love yourself and can present with enthusiasm. The *Better Homes and Gardens Story Book* (Meredith Publishing Company, Des Moines, Iowa) contains a wonderful selection of the most dearly loved children's stories.

The *Sunday Times* (London) has published an incomparable pamphlet, *The One Hundred Best Books for Children,* giving dates of first publication, the age group that will most enjoy each book, and a brief description and evaluation of each book. All books listed are in print; they have been chosen by the *Sunday Times* working in association with Miss Katherine Lines, author of *Four to Fourteen: A Library of Books for Children.* Any well-stocked children's library will have this pamphlet. It can be ordered from London (1/6) or from a New York bookstore for about fifty cents. It is undoubtedly the finest list of imaginative, stimulating, literary books available.

As the first selection for an intelligent high-school or college student there is nothing as good as the introductory essay in Paul Haines's *Problems in Prose*.[1] It is an entertaining and illuminating essay on reading, written for college students, and will prove equally valuable for any teacher of remedial reading.

There is a great deal of talk about rapid reading. This will come naturally with practice to the child who starts out with a firm basis in phonics. It is generally said that wide reading in easy books is necessary to develop speed, but actually reading a favorite book a second and perhaps a third time will produce speed and fluency faster than anything else. Another method of gaining speed is for the student to force himself to read just a little faster than is comfortable and presently he will find that this faster speed has become comfortable. Another help is a stop watch. Boys particularly like anything mechanical, and if they are allowed to time themselves with a watch and find out how long it takes for the first ten pages and the next ten pages, they will often double their speed in a surprisingly short time. Of course, no one should try to read rapidly until he has first learned to read accurately. One's speed in reading depends on the type of material read, and people who abhor fiction and like science never do become fast readers.

[1] A Foreword to the Student, pp. xxi–xxviii, Harper & Brothers, New York, fourth edition, 1957.

Twelve / Phonics in Action: Sound and Sense
A Briefing for the Teacher

The first question that may come to your mind is, "Who needs phonics?" The answer is, "Anyone who cannot instantly read any word or nonsense syllable, anyone who reads very slowly, anyone who has trouble with spelling." Also, very likely, the student who is not getting as good grades in school as his intelligence would warrant. His difficulty may lie elsewhere, but phonics and reading are the first things to check.

The simplest test for a child is to ask him to read a page out loud and see if he stumbles over the words. An older student may have learned most words as sight words and yet not know phonics, so give him a brief test of nonsense syllables, such as:

pleroid ploy sprute gril Zephaniah treopat ropping

To help you teach this phonics system, here is a simple guide to the lessons that follow: First you are asked to learn to pronounce forty sounds clearly and with assurance, and to become familiar with the phonetic symbols used here, which are given on page 170. To learn these sounds, start by pronouncing the key words, and then abstracting the sounds from them and saying them by themselves.

Notice that the letters are printed in boldface type and

the phonetic symbols (representing sounds) in italics. **Ch** in boldface is a digraph which can be pronounced three ways (**chair, machine, school**), while *ch* in italics represents just one sound, that found at the beginning and end of **church.**

Consonant sounds should properly be whispered, because if you say them aloud you must perforce add a vowel sound, so that **b** becomes "buh," and so on. Actually, in practice, it may be helpful to explain this to the child and then let him say "buh," "cuh," "duh," loudly and firmly. The extra noise reinforces the learning. This slight distortion of the sound does not seem to cause trouble in sounding out words.

Many children have been taught to say the consonant sounds improperly by teachers who were not trained in this simple procedure of extracting sounds from words. Retarded readers commonly pronounce **l** as "ell" instead of "luh," and **r** as "er" instead of "ruh." Then **like** and **rat** become two-syllable horrors, "ell-ike" and "er-at." Often it is necessary to explain to the child that the sound a letter makes is not the same as its name. **B** says "buh" not "bee."

You will notice that in the list of consonant sounds **c, q,** and **x** are not included. These superfluous letters do not represent additional sounds but duplicate the sounds of other letters. The letter **c** is pronounced either *s* or *k*, **qu** as *kw,* and **x** as *ks.*

The sixteen vowel sounds, in contrast with the consonants, may be said out loud, shouted if you like. The only ones that offer any difficulty are the short vowel sounds, which are the most frequently used but which we are the least aware of by themselves.

In speaking of these sounds to your student, call them "long **a**," or the "long **a** sound," or $\bar{a}$ (making the sound), "long **e**" or $\bar{e}$, and the "short **a**" or $\breve{a}$. Similarly, you may speak of the "**b** sound" or *b* (making the sound), the "**d** sound" or *d,* the "long **oo** sound" or $\bar{oo}$.

THE SOUNDS AND THEIR SYMBOLS

5 long vowel sounds

$\bar{a}$ ate
$\bar{e}$ be
$\bar{i}$ ice
$\bar{o}$ bone
$\bar{u}$ use

5 short vowel sounds

$\breve{a}$ at
$\breve{e}$ egg
$\breve{i}$ it
$\breve{o}$ on
$\breve{u}$ up

6 special vowel sounds

$\overline{oo}$ shoot
$\breve{oo}$ book
oy boy
aw paw
ou ouch
$\dot{a}$ ah!

18 consonant sounds

b big
d dog
f fun
g go
h hat
j jump
k kind
l like
m me
n no
p pet
r run
s see
t tell
v very
w will
y you
z zero

6 special consonant sounds

th the, thin
ch child
sh she
zh treasure
ng sing
hw where

In the same way, practice the sounds of the following consonant combinations called the "blends." With monotonous regularity children with reading problems mispronounce them as independent syllables because they have been taught to do so. **Br** becomes **bur; cr, cur; pl, pul; sn, sun,** etc., and **play** is read as "pul-ay." Instead, say "bruh," "cruh," etc.

The blends, of course, are not new sounds but combinations of the ones already learned. However, they are said so close together that they seem like new sounds and should be learned as separate entities.

The blends in the left-hand column would be represented phonetically by the same letters printed in italics, thus, *br, cl,* etc. There are nine exceptions, all containing **c** or **qu.** These sounds are represented by phonetic symbols in parentheses.

THE CONSONANT BLENDS

br	bring	gl	glow
cr *(kr)*	crack	pl	play
fr	from	sl	slow
dr	drink	spl	splash
gr	grow	sc *(s)*	scent
pr	pretty	sc *(sk)*	scat
tr	try	sch *(sk)*	school
chr *(kr)*	chrome	sk	sky
scr *(skr)*	scrap	sm	small
shr	shriek	sn	snow
spr	spring	sp	spot
str	string	squ *(skw)*	squaw
thr	throw	st	stop
bl	blue	sw	swing
cl *(kl)*	clean	tw	twin
fl	flap		

There is one more phonetic symbol used, and it is ə. It is called the *schwa* and stands for the neutral vowel sound found in unaccented syllables. In the words **bag, beg, big, bog,** and **bug** each vowel has its distinctive sound, but the **a** in **about,** the **e** in **taken,** the **i** in **pencil,** the **o** in **lemon,** and the **u** in **circus** are all shortened up to sound approximately the same and all are represented by ə (as in ə*bout, irel-*əv*ənt*). "Buh," "duh," and "cuh" referred to earlier should be written *b*ə, *d*ə, and *k*ə. The concept of the schwa is mentioned for the sake of accuracy and because the student will encounter it if he consults a dictionary. It explains much of our trouble with spelling. Since so many vowels are pronounced alike, we cannot always guess the spelling of a word from its sound.

The phonetic symbols printed throughout the material serve the purpose of focusing the student's attention on the sounds and help him identify them in the words he speaks and reads.

This is a simplified phonic system and differs from those in the dictionaries as follows: (1) Only one **th** sound is given (there are really two, as in **the** and **thin,** but it is not necessary to teach both to beginners. Just say, "For **th** you put your tongue between your teeth."; (2) the *hw* sound (written **wh,** as in **when**) is listed as a separate sound, whereas it is really a "blend"; and (3) two additional sounds have been omitted, both of which occur before the letter **r.** The words **air, bear, care, their,** etc., are listed here with the *ā* words; **here, beer, fierce, fear,** etc., with the *ē* words. Webster's *New World Dictionary* represents the vowels in these words by *â* and *ê*, but says they are pronounced in various ways, of which *ā* and *ē* are two. This is explained for the sake of accuracy, but don't bother the children with it.

Owing to the fact that there are more than forty sounds and only twenty-six letters, many of the letters are pronounced in more than one way and some sounds are represented by two letters. To further complicate things, all the long vowel sounds and many of the other sounds are regularly spelled in more than one way. All this will become clear as you go through the system.

There are two reasons for our mixed-up system of spelling. One is that English has borrowed words from many other languages. The other is that, historically, pronunciation has changed faster than spelling. "One" used to be pronounced in two syllables about the way a southerner would say "owner." In English there are a large number of homonyms, or words which sound alike but have different meanings, for example, **gait** and **gate, wait** and **weight, read** and **reed.** It is a great advantage to have them spelled differently because the reader then knows at once which one is meant.

Do not be afraid that you do not know enough phonics to teach it. The happiest teaching situation is where you and the student are making discoveries together. Every step is explained in detail and will be easy to follow. Unless you are an experienced teacher of remedial reading, you will probably learn a good deal that is new to you about the spelling of so-called nonphonetic words, which follow a more regular system than most people realize. You may want to skim through the system before you start teaching it. In any case, it is recommended that you read the few pages of the advanced part so that you can see what kinds of mistakes are made and what sorts of difficulties are encountered by students who have been taught reading and spelling without the proper background in phonics.

The second way to prepare yourself to teach is to try to divest yourself of the idea that because your student has had trouble in reading and spelling he is not bright. It cannot be too strongly emphasized that no matter how poor his reading and spelling, this is not in itself any sign that he is unintelligent. One of the author's first cases was a boy who had attended school for five years and still could read nothing except **ing.** Yet he had a high I.Q. and, once started properly, learned to read rapidly.

You must convey to your student the idea that he is normal and that it is not his fault that he has had difficulty. Simply tell him that he was not taught properly. A child who has been trained in phonics and reading, but who is left with the feeling that he lacks some ability which other children have, will often still remain a problem and will not have the courage to use what he has learned.

The general teaching procedure is simple. At first the student is simply asked to repeat sounds after the teacher while looking at the letters on the page. Thus, an association is set up between the sounds and the letters. You will not have to drill him on these sounds over and over until he knows them all perfectly. Indeed, you are to tell him he does not have to memorize all these things. It is sufficient if he can read a line or two at a time after you. The first five pages are a preview of the whole system—the twenty-six letters, forty sounds, thirty-nine digraphs, and twenty-nine blends. On the next two pages he reads consonants and vowels combined into syllables. It is not necessary to show him how to blend letters. Simply pronounce the combinations, have him pronounce them after you, and he will understand how this blending is done.

The first two columns on the A/a page will be a struggle. After that he will be able to read the next phonograms on the A/a page and the words on the A page by himself. The rest of this system will go rapidly. It is not a matter of teaching and drilling over and over again. It becomes simply a matter of having the student read what is on the page.

As for timing, it works out best if you go through the system rapidly in half-hour or hour lessons. Even children as young as seven or eight can spend an hour at a time without becoming tired. By going through this period of concentrated rapid work, instead of stretching it out over weeks or months, the child has a feeling of suddenly getting insight into what it's all about. Thus, after three or four days' work he changes from a state of apathy or despair to one of courage and confidence. It cannot be stressed too much that you must maintain a good steady pace and move along with speed and enthusiasm, without requiring memorizing of the first steps. All the items on the first six pages are repeated over and over again, and there is no danger of their not being learned by the time you finish.

Now for the first step. The best way to begin with a little fellow who seems to have no ability in attacking a new word is to turn first to the long words on pages 252 and 253 and ask, "What do you do when you come to a new word you don't know? How do you sound it out?", and then don't wait for an answer, but say, "Let's read this first word here." Start with **kangaroo,** divided into syllables, and say, "What does **k** say?" If he doesn't answer, say, "**k** says 'kuh,' and **a-n-g** says 'ang,' so that makes **kang. A** says 'uh' and **r** says 'ruh' and **oo** says o̅o̅, so that makes 'aroo.' Now let's put it all together, **kangaroo.** You know what a **kangaroo** is don't you? Now you read it twice carefully while you look at the syllables, **kangaroo, kangaroo.** Now read the word here where it is written together, not divided up. Good! Now you will remember that word, and you can read it any time you meet it." And he *will* be able to read it next day and any day. He will have associated the letters, the sounds, and the meaning, and the word will have become a meaningful unit which he can recognize at a glance.

If he is interested you can teach him another word or two. For an older child who has a fairly sizable stock of sight words and knows some phonics, but gives up on long words, you may take one of the harder words down on the page, such as **concentrating,** and work through that. An astonishing number of children trained to look at the first of the word or the last of the word or the two tall things sticking up in the middle actually do not know that sounds go all the way through a word, and none of them have any idea of syllables, but they get this idea by being helped to sound out one or two words.

Perhaps your student has had a little phonics and starts sounding out the first syllable of **concentrating** by saying *k-ŏ-n* and then painfully combining them into **con.** Then when he starts reading the word again he goes through this whole process a second time. Explain that, "You did it just right. *k-ŏ-n* makes **con,** but you don't sound the syllable out a second time; that is only for the first time you read it. Once you sound it out, *k-ŏ-n,* then you just read it a couple of times, saying **con,** and then you know the first syllable of **concentrating** and you never have to sound it out again." Then show him that **con** is not only the beginning of **concentrating** but that it occurs in lots of other words. Show him **container** and **conversation** on the same page. Point out that once he has learned the **con** in **concentrating,** he will know that syllable wherever he meets it and it will help him in reading dozens of other words. Take the dictionary and show him how many words start with **con.** Put the word **concentrating** in a sentence or two so you are sure he is aware of the meaning, not just of the sounds.

If he gets the idea and is interested, you may want to teach him other words from this page in the same way, and show him that the same syllables occur over and over again in different words. **Tion, ment,** and **trans** are in a great many words, so once he has learned them, he can read them right off wherever he sees them.

This same procedure should be used with an advanced student. Get him to try difficult words he does not know, perhaps those on page 254 or some in the dictionary. Tell him to start at the left and keep going until he comes out at the other end. He should read by syllables rather than by individual letters.

It may be possible to introduce the basic idea of spelling right here for this older child. After he has read one of the words by syllables twice and then as a whole once or twice, you may cover the word and say, "Now write it," and he will find to his surprise that he can write it correctly. Tell him to say the syllables as he writes them, not the letters.

This is a description of how gifted children seem to teach themselves reading and spelling without any effort. The first time they meet a word they spend a little time going through it from left to right by syllables, pronounce it as a whole, become aware of its meaning, and from then on recognize it instantly. After a few hours spent on this phonics system, any child will have acquired this knack. "Reading by syllables" does not mean that you divide a word into syllables before you start to read it. Rather you just start at the left and keep going, and the sounds fall into syllables of their own accord.

You may not believe it can all be this simple, but it is. The problem reader and speller, not having been taught the right method of learning to read and spell a word, has been using totally inadequate methods, some of which he has been taught and some of which he developed on his own. One little boy, confronted with the word **knew,** said brightly, "I know, you look at the end of the word and then you say the k!" Many children try to teach themselves their spelling lessons by reciting the letters of each word over and over in a sort of rhythmic chant, disregarding syllables. To learn **succeed,** for instance, after one hasty glance at the word, they gaze off into the corner of the room and say over and over **s-u c-c e-e d.** They are attempting the impossible task of memorizing a nonsense pattern of sounds instead of words, and these sound patterns desert them on the Friday test.

After this preliminary lesson on long words, the next step is to check up and see whether your student really knows all the letters of the alphabet well enough to name and print them. A typical retarded reader is still confusing **b, d, p,** and **q,** and perhaps **m, n,** and **w,** at the age of ten. You can show him that these first four letters are really all the same shape but are written in different positions, and it is the position that is important. Also **s** and **c** must face the right way. This is the first and essential step in eliminating "poor visual imagery" and a tendency to make reversals.

Now you are ready to go ahead. Equip yourself with a pencil for pointing, some paper for writing out sample words, and a dictionary. You will find this work will stimulate curiosity about words and spelling, and you will refer to the dictionary often.

One last point may be made. Some of the brighter and more advanced students will start challenging the system, the rules, and the teacher. They ask questions and bring up exceptions with great gusto. This is a fine and healthy sign and should be encouraged. Get such students to go through the dictionary and make up their own rules. Let them try to find a rule for the sound of g before e, i, and y, for instance. They will learn fast this way. For younger students, it is better to avoid mention of exceptions and just state, in answer to questions, "We take that up later on."

All that remains is to follow the time-honored custom of beginning teachers the world over, namely, keep one page ahead of the class!

Teaching and Learning

STEP-BY-STEP INSTRUCTIONS
FOR TEACHER AND STUDENT

THE CONSONANTS

page 211

To the Student

Let us begin with the consonants. I don't expect you to remember all of these things, just to be able to repeat them after me. We'll come back to them all one at a time.

Here at the top of the page are the consonants. There are two c's, two g's, and two s's because these letters have two sounds, and the q is followed by a u because it always is in English.

See if you can tell me the sounds these letters make.

For the Teacher

Probably your student will know the b sound, but not the two sounds for c. If he hesitates at all or makes any sounds incorrectly, take over and from then on you say the sounds and have him say them after you while looking at the letters. If he is quite uncertain, do three or four at a time; if he knows most of them, you can do a whole line at a time. He should end by being able to say all the consonant sounds once without help.

Say *k* and *s* for c, *g* and *j* for g, *s* and *z* for s. Be sure to say them clearly. Pointing with your pencil, show that the sounds of the first c and the k are the same, the sounds of the second c and the first s are the same, the second g sounds the same as j, and so on. Don't at this point try to show the student any written words starting with these letters unless he specifically asks you to. We want to focus his attention only on the sound and the letters at this point. You should, however, say a word beginning with b, such as bat, and pause and give him a chance to offer another word, and so on for the other letters. Most children have learned

181

to do this in school for a few initial consonants and enjoy showing what they know. (Examples: **qu** in **quick**; x in **tax**; z sound for s in **is**.)

R U L E 1
page 211

For the Teacher

Read the rule at the bottom of the page slowly, pointing to the letters and words. Have the student read the sample words. He need not memorize the rule.

T H E   V O W E L S
page 212

To the Student

You know the names of the vowels **a, e, i, o, u,** and sometimes **y.** All vowels have more than one sound. The long vowels says their own names, so they are very easy to learn. You just say $\bar{a}, \bar{e}, \bar{\imath}, \bar{o}, \bar{u}.$ **y** is pronounced $\bar{\imath}$, just like the letter **i** when it is a long vowel. Below the vowels it shows how we write these sounds. The letters are in italics. Each has a straight line over it. That means it is not the letter **a,** but the long $\bar{a}$ sound. Now you read the long vowels.

Next we have the short vowel sounds and they are hard little sounds to learn because, while you have said them millions of times, you have almost never said them alone since you were a tiny baby. In words they are nearly always said with one or more consonants.

In the picture you see a very lazy, fat boy by the name of Ed who is not up yet. Under the picture it says "Fat Ed is not up." Each one of these words has one of the short vowel sounds in it—$\breve{a}, \breve{e}, \breve{\imath}, \breve{o}, \breve{u}.$ If you try to say "Fat Ed is

not up" with your mouth wide open, you will hear yourself
say the short vowel sounds. We write these short sounds as
letters with little curves over them. When y is a short vowel,
it is sounded just like short **i.**

For the Teacher

Have the student repeat the sentence after you with his
mouth open a couple of times. Then, have him say the same
sounds again while looking at the vowels below the sentence,
saying ĭ for **y.** It may take a little practice to keep the lips
relaxed so no consonant sound is made.

To the Student

At the bottom of the page we have one more sound for
a as in **ah.** The sound is written **a** with a dot over it. (*ȧ*)

For the Teacher

It is not intended that you drill the student so that he
knows all of these sounds and can give them perfectly when
called upon. They are difficult to learn in isolation, and a
student has great trouble distinguishing between ĕ and ĭ. It
is sufficient to go over them a few times until he becomes
aware of what they sound like and can repeat the series
after you while looking at the letters. He will learn them
later.

SPECIAL VOWEL SOUNDS
page 213

To the Student

Next we have the special vowel sounds. These are sounds
written with two letters, and there are little pictures down

below to help you remember what the sounds are. Notice there are two sounds for **oo**. Three of these sounds are written two ways.

The long **oo** sound says $\bar{oo}$, as in **boot**, and the short **oo** sound says $\breve{oo}$, as in **book**. Then there is **ou**. If someone hurts you, you say *ou; oy* is the sound in **boy**, and *aw* is the sound in **paw**. In italics we have the ways of writing these sounds. Can you say some words with $\bar{oo}$ and $\breve{oo}$? Now you read them.

For the Teacher

Read the sounds one at a time and have your student repeat them after you two or three times, while looking at the letters, until he can say all five in sequence. Then cover the pictures and have him say them again. Of course, the $\bar{oo}$ and $\breve{oo}$ sounds are also sometimes spelled in other ways as we shall see later. (Example: **through, put**)

SPECIAL CONSONANT SOUNDS
page 213

To the Student

Now we have five more special sounds to learn. These are consonant sounds that have to be written with two letters. **ng** comes only at the end of a word, and **wh** at the beginning of a word. The rest can come at the beginning or the end. The pictures will help you remember them. *th* is the beginning sound in **thimble**, *ch* is the beginning sound in **chick**, and *sh* is the beginning sound in **ship**, and *ng* is the end sound in **ring**. *hw* is the sound beginning **wheel**. Now say the sounds after me while you look at the letters.

VOWEL DIGRAPHS

page 214

To the Student

Next we have vowel digraphs, that is, vowel sounds written with two letters. We have learned the long vowel sounds on page 212. These same long vowel sounds, $\bar{a}$, $\bar{e}$, $\bar{i}$, $\bar{o}$, $\bar{u}$, are all written in other ways with two vowels together. When you see these vowel combinations, remember they generally say the long sound of the first letter, so they are easy. (Tell the more advanced student that there are many exceptions as we shall see.)

For the Teacher

Point to the phonograms in the first column and read $\bar{a}$, $\bar{a}$, $\bar{a}$ (ai as in **wait**; **ay** as in **say**). Then see if the student can carry on for the next four columns. If not, help him.

Have him repeat the rule after you, "These generally say the long sound of the first letter."

If the student asks for examples, you might use these: **see, sea, pie, oat, toe, snow, true,** and **fruit.**

To the Student

At the bottom on the page we see more vowel digraphs. **ei** says the long a sound, $\bar{a}$, which is a surprise. Also, in some words it says the long e sound, $\bar{e}$. **ie** says $\bar{i}$, as you saw above, but it sometimes also says $\bar{e}$. **ew** and **eu** say the long u sound, $\bar{u}$, or $\bar{oo}$.

For the Teacher

Some examples are: **eight, receive, pie, believe, few,** and **feud.**

All these digraphs are single vowel sounds occurring within a syllable. The **ie** in **salient** is not a digraph, of course, since the **i** and **e** are in different syllables.

VOWELS FOLLOWED BY R

page 214

To the Student

Next we have the vowels followed by **r**. When a vowel is followed by **r**, it has a different sound than it has when it is followed by any other letter; so we learn the sounds of these combinations.

The ones in the first line, **er, ir, ur**, all say exactly the same thing—**er**, as in **her**. Then **or** is just the word **or**, and there is **ar** as in **car**. The **a** in **ar** is that last **a** sound, *à*. Now you read them.

For the Teacher

Read the words and put each in a sentence or phrase. "I see **her**." "The **fir** tree." "A **fur** coat." "You **or** me." etc. (The vowel sound in **er** is the *ə*; in **or** it is *aw*.)

RULE 2

page 214

To the Student

Here we have the second rule that you have to learn that will help you with hundreds of words.

When you have one vowel followed by one consonant, the vowel has the short sound, *ă*. If there is an **e** after the consonant, the **e** is silent and does not say anything, but it makes the first vowel say its long sound, *ā*.

For the Teacher

Recite the rule very slowly and distinctly pointing to the **a** and **t** in **at.** Then point to the **e** in **ate,** then to the **a.** Then repeat **at** and **ate,** emphasizing the vowel sounds.

Read the columns vertically—**at, ate, et, ete, it, ite,** etc. Explain that, except for **at, it,** and **ate,** these are not words, they are the ends of words and syllables. Examples of words with these phonograms are:

| at | pet | kit | not | cut |
| ate | Pete | kite | note | cute |

First read **at** and **ate** and have the student repeat those; then go on to the others, one pair at a time. Then read them all over and see if he can read them all correctly.

The rule need not be learned by heart. It is used simply as an explanation. For young children do not call attention to the printed rule on the page. Older people may want to read it for themselves.

CONSONANT BLENDS

page 215

To the Student

On this page we have what we call the consonant blends. Now these are the same letters and the same sounds you have had before, but they are said so close together that they sound like new sounds. I will read the first column to you and you say them after me.

For the Teacher

Do not write out any words unless asked, but say some words beginning with the consonant blends, such as **bread,**

cry, fry, and encourage the student to suggest some words himself. Be sure that you say the **tr** as in **trap** and show the student that it is not like **tur** as in **turn** or **Turk.** Go over half a dozen sounds at a time and let the student repeat them after you until he can do so perfectly. There are two **sc** sounds, *s* and *sk*, as in **scent** and **scat.**

You are trying here to have your student become aware of these sounds as entities that exist in the words he speaks.

The blends with **r** are the most important and most difficult. If further work seems called for, say the words below in pairs and ask the student to tell which starts with the *g* sound and which with the *gr* sound, etc.

girl	grill
bite	bright
cane	crane
dawn	drawn
fight	fright
go	grow
tack	track

To the Student

chr says *kr*, and **sch** says *sk*. (The **h** in both of these is silent, as in **chrome** and **school.**)

ODD WAYS OF WRITING SOME CONSONANT SOUNDS

page 216

To the Student

Next we have some peculiar things. Each one is made up of two consonants with special ways of sounding them that you would never guess. In the first four, **wr, kn, gn,** and **ps,** the first letter is silent, so they all just have the sound of the second letter, *r, n, n*, and *s*. The **ph** sounds like the letter **f**, *f*, and the **gh** is a particular demon. Mostly it does not say anything at all, it is just put in to make spelling difficult, but sometimes it says the f sound, *f*, and sometimes the g sound, *g*. Now you read them.

Just to make this complete, we are going to put in some unusual things here. In **rh** the h is silent, and you say *r*, **gu** says *g*. **Ti, si,** and **ci** you will meet later in hard words where they all say *sh*, but do not worry about them now. (They can also have the sounds of *tĭ, sĭ*, and *sĭ*, as in **partition, transition,** and **precision.**)

For the Teacher

Examples of words with these digraphs are: **write, know, gnaw, psychic, phone, though, cough, ghost, rhyme, guard, station, mission, special.**

To the Student

Now we have one last thing: **le** says *əl*. This little upside-down e stands for a very short vowel sound. All of the vowels are pronounced this way sometimes. For instance, in **lemon,** the **o** is shortened up so you really don't hear it as a short **o** sound at all.

These syllables occur at the ends of words. **ble** says *bəl*, as in **table**; **cle** says *kəl*, as in **circle.**

For the Teacher

The **le** is the only instance besides **wh** (*hw*) where sounds are written backward. Otherwise all words are read from left to right.

Read these syllables to the student and have him repeat them after you. If he asks for further examples, they are to be found in: **ladle, baffle, struggle, tackle, apple, rassle, little,** and **dazzle.**

To the Student

Believe it or not, now you have covered the whole field of phonics. You have learned all the sounds (except *zh*) and all the ways of writing the sounds, and you have learned the two important rules. These are all the "bricks" with which our words are built. The hard part is over. The rest is just practice combining the parts you have already had.

COMBINING A CONSONANT
WITH LONG AND SHORT VOWELS

page 217

To the Student

Here we are going to start combining one consonant with one vowel. Most of the things here are not words (although there are one or two words like **he** and **be**), but they are beginnings of words and separate syllables in longer words; so these will help you to read and write thousands of words. These must be read both with a long vowel and with a short vowel sound.

This page sounds very silly when you read it out loud, but at least it is easy, so let's do it.

For the Teacher

Read the first line with *ā, rā, wā,* and so on, and have the child repeat it after you; do the same with the second line. Then repeat, using short vowel sounds, and be sure you say the short *ă* sound, as in **at**, clearly and distinctly and have the child repeat it. On this page he really begins to learn those long and short vowel sounds as well as to use the consonants with ease. Go on through the rest of the page, first with the long vowel sounds and then with the short ones. Most children will need a good deal of help on the first two lines and be quite fluent by the time they reach the last two.

Be sure to say the soft c (s) before e and i, and the hard c (k) before a, o, and u.

COMBINING A BLEND
WITH LONG AND SHORT VOWELS
page 217

To the Student

Now we are going to read the blends that you learned earlier followed by a vowel. Like the combination on the last page, these must be read with both the long and short vowels. These things are not words, but beginnings of words or syllables and, of course, they will help you with thousands of words and syllables.

For the Teacher

On this page we do exactly the same thing but we use the blends instead of the single consonants and have the child read them with both long and short sounds. First *trā, drā, crā*, etc., and then *tră, dră, cră*, as in **trap, drab, crab**, etc.

A/a
page 219

For the Teacher

On this page we really get into the heart of the system. The first column with a followed by the consonants, starting with five familiar words, is perfectly simple for the child with no reading problem and very difficult for the remedial reading case. One and all—whether five or forty, even though they have been reading for years and have graduated from college—will have the greatest difficulty with it. Here's where the reversals come in—they want to say **ta** instead of **at.** Frequently they act as though they were going to choke to death over a short vowel. An hour's work should clear up this page.

Say to the child, "In this first column we have a followed by all the different consonants. When we have one vowel followed by one consonant in a word, the vowel has a short sound. In the second column you have exactly the same thing as in the first column with an **e** on the end, and, as you know, the **e** is silent but the **a** has its long sound—*ăt*, *āte*. Let us first read down the first column."

Read slowly and distinctly **at** so that he hears distinctly the *ă* and the *t* sounds, **am, an,** and then let him go ahead on his own. There is a little dot in front of the **ag** and the **ac.** That is to help him remember that **g** and **c** have the hard sound in the first column and the soft sound in the second column. The **s** in the first column is pronounced *z* and the second column we will read with the *z* sound, though occasionally -**se** is pronounced *s*. **al** is pronounced as in **pal.** **ar** is in parentheses because it has the sound of **ar,** as in **car. are** is pronounced as in **bare,** not as in the word **are.** Once you have struggled through the first column, do the second column, which will be much, much easier. Then read across— **at, ate, am, ame.** This is one place where you must drill until the child can do it fluently and easily with no hesitation.

Now go on to the next column and explain that the **a**'s are all short, except in the last three combinations which are marked long. Show that these columns have the same letters as the first column on the page, plus one or two more consonants. These are all the *ends* of syllables which are found in hundreds and hundreds of words. The child who learned the first column perfectly will have no difficulty at all with these two. The last three combinations with the **a** marked long come from **change, paste,** and **bathe.** In the last column, **ank** has a slightly nasal sound, as in **bank,** and **ang** you hear in **sang. al** can be pronounced either *al*, as in the first column, or *awl*, as in the words **already, salt,** and **all.** The last nine combinations consist of the sound of **ar** plus another consonant. The last one is the end of the word **large.**

A WORDS

page 220

To the Student

Here we have 152 words which you can now read. There is an **a** in each word, and you will be able to tell whether you pronounce it with its long or short sound. These words are just the same things you had on the page before, except that you have one or two consonants at the beginning. You can read them.

For the Teacher

Have the student read these words. Even a little fellow who could read almost nothing before starting this work will be able to read them by himself with very little help.

See that he notices when he starts the **ar** words. If any mistakes are made, it will be in leaving out **r**'s which should be there, or putting them in where they don't belong. If a mistake is made, point to the word with your pencil and ask him to try again.

This page may look dull but it is a very exciting moment when a little boy suddenly finds he can read 152 words on his own with no help from pictures or context. When you finish this page you are about halfway through the system in point of time. The rest will go much faster. Many children will want to start reading at this point.

To the Student

Now you can read any one-syllable word in the English langauge with **a** for a vowel and all of the syllables of all the other words that have **a** for a vowel. You will find the rest of the work will be much easier.

E/e

page 222

To the Student

Next you have the letter **e**. Just as on the A page, the first column has **e** followed by every one of the consonants. The second column is the same with the silent **e** on the end, which makes the first **e** long. Remember again that the **c** and **g** change their sounds in the second column when they are followed by **e** and that **er** has a different sound from the rest.

E WORDS

page 223

To the Student

Now you can read all the one-syllable words with **e** for a vowel and all the syllables in all the other words that have **e** for a vowel.

For the Teacher

Proceed as with the A page. This one will go much more easily. It is interesting that there are few monosyllables in

English in which ē is spelled e-consonant-e. Most are spelled with **ea** or **ee.**

I/i

page 224

The two I pages which follow will be taught just like the A and E pages.

Notice again that **g** and **c** change their sounds between the first and second columns, that **ir** is a special sound, and also notice the long ī in **ild** and **ind.** These represent important "families" and should be learned. Here a single vowel is long before two consonants. **ind** is also pronounced with a short **i** (ĭ).

O/o

page 227

Notice the long **o** in **old, olt** and **ost,** and that the last three items have the *aw* sound, as in **soft, boss,** and **cost.** Your English friends will pronounce **cost** with ŏ as *kŏst.* **of** should be pronounced ŏf as in **doff,** not like the word **of,** which is ŭv.

U/u

page 230

On the U/u page, **ull** is printed twice. Note the different sounds in **pull** and **hull.** The **u** in **pull** says ŏŏ, not ŭ.

Y/y

page 233

To the Student

The Y page you will find very easy. **y** is just like **i** when it is used as a vowel. When it comes at the end of a syllable or of a short one-syllable word it has the sound of *i*. As a suffix or ending to a word, it has the sound you hear in **party**. Sometimes it is used in a syllable where it is followed by a consonant, and then it has the *i* sound, just as though the syllable were spelled with an **i**.

For the Teacher

These are the first words of more than one syllable. If necessary help him read one syllable at a time by covering up the end of the word and exposing only the first syllable, then the second, etc. Then have him read the whole word by syllables. Of course, put the words in sentences where necessary.

WORDS WITH
VOWEL DIGRAPHS

page 234

To the Student

On this page we start with the vowel digraphs which we first met on page 214. Remember they say the long sound of the first letter, so they are actually just a different way of writing the long vowel sounds. Following the **ai** we have some phonograms which are **ai** followed by another consonant, and the same for **oa** and **ee**. When you have read these, you can read the words at the bottom of the page. Listen as you do so to the long vowel sounds.

ea has three sounds

page 235

For the Teacher

Continue with the digraphs on pages 235 and 236. There are only a few **ea** words in which the **ea** is pronounced $\bar{a}$, and the student should learn them right here. Explain that **ea** is pronounced not only "like the long sound of the first letter," but also like the long sound of the second letter and like the short sound of the first letter. This is true of other vowel digraphs, to a lesser extent, and is a more accurate rule than the one quoted above which is a simplification used for beginners.

With words like **read** and **tear**, which have two pronunciations, we cannot tell which one is meant unless we read the word in a sentence.

To the Student

When you come to a new word with **ea** in it, you may have to try both the long and short sounds of **e.**

The next five digraphs are easy. In these words **ow** says $\bar{o}$. It also sometimes says *ou* as we shall see later. **ie** more often says $\bar{e}$ than $\bar{\imath}$.

$$\left.\begin{matrix} \text{ei} \\ \text{ey} \end{matrix}\right\} \text{say } \bar{e} \text{ or } \bar{a}$$

page 237

For the Teacher

ei comes within syllables and **ey** at the end of words.

Have the student learn to write the word **eight.** This will help him recognize this odd group of letters whenever he sees it. Point out the silent **gh**. (**Height** and **sleight** are exceptions in which **eigh** says *ī*.)

To the Student

Once you know that *ā* is a regular way of pronouncing **ei** and **ey**, the spelling of many words will seem reasonable.

Remember that **cei** always says *sē*. Then you can spell **receive** and other demons.

SPECIAL VOWEL SOUNDS
page 238

To the Student

There are two ways of writing the *ou* sound: **ou** is always within a word; **ow** at the end of a word and sometimes inside a word.

Here we have two ways of writing the *aw* sound: **aw** comes at the end of a word and sometimes within a word; **au** is always within a word. As you know, the word **all** has the same *aw* sound.

There are two ways of writing the *oy* sound. **oy** is generally used at the end of the word and **oi** in the middle of the word. You can always count on these two to say the same thing.

(The following paragraph may be omitted for the beginner.) The *ōō* and *ū* sounds are really very much alike. In fact, *ū* sounds the same as *ōō*, except that it starts with the **y** consonant sound. Most of us don't distinguish between the two sounds in many of the words. In the first group, **oo** is pronounced *ōō*. In the second and third columns, **ew** and **ue** are sometimes pronounced *ōō* and sometimes *ū*. **Cue** has the *ū* sound, and **true** has the *ōō* sound; **grew** is *ōō*, and **knew** is *ū*. We point this out for accuracy's sake. As far as reading goes, you can forget it. You will just say these words so they sound right to you. Of course, **Tuesday** should be pronounced with a *ū* and not "Toosday."

The *ŏŏ* sound is written also with a **u.**

ODD WAYS OF WRITING SOME CONSONANT SOUNDS

Three curiosities with silent first letters

page 240

To the Student

Now we are going to study three curiosities. They are the consonant digraphs **kn, wr,** and **gn;** and in all of them the first letter is silent and the second letter is sounded. We have to learn these because they come in so many very common words. **kn** and **wr** always occur at the beginning of words or syllables.

Right now is a good time to take a hard look at **gn,** which is always pronounced *n*—the g being silent. It comes at the beginning and at the end of words or syllables. There are only a few common words beginning with **gn,** and we should have no trouble just remembering to read them as though the g weren't there. When **gn** occurs at the end of a word or syllable, it still has the **n** sound, and you might think it would be just as well to leave out that silent g. Actually, it seems to have a use in some words like **sign** and **align,** because it changes the vowel sound from short to long. That is, s-i-n is **sin** and s-i-g-n is **sign.** Of course, in **reign** and **campaign,** the vowel sound would be long anyway. If you will become perfectly familiar with the sight and sound of **gn,** it will help you to learn to spell a lot of hard words which would otherwise seem baffling.

For the Teacher

The only excuse for these three complications seems to be that they are used in writing homonyms: we have **know** and **no; knew** and **new; write** and **right; wrap** and **rap;** and we have names like **Nat, Nome,** and **Nash** that are to be distinguished from **gnat, gnome,** and **gnash.** Explain this if it seems appropriate.

The beginner need read only the easier words and need not be bothered with all of the above explanation.

Four more curiosities

pages 240–241

To the Student

Now for **rh,** which is pronounced *r.* Remember that the h is silent. **rh** is found in words that come from Greek stems. Like the other demons on this and the preceding page, it is perfectly simple to learn if you just face it squarely. Learn to recognize it when you see it, and it will enable you to read many words which would otherwise seem impossible. (*For the teacher:* In fact, it may even enable you to learn to spell two of the most difficult words in the English language: **hemorrhage** and **diarrhea.**)

gu always has the *g* sound.

To go on with our demons and oddities, we have another one that we inherited from the Greeks—**ph,** which is always pronounced *f.* It occurs both at the beginnings and ends of words and syllables. We run into it in a great many words which scientists and engineers made up from two Greek roots: **phone,** which means "sound," and **graph,** which means "write," as in **telephone, telegraph, phonograph,** etc. Learn **ph** and you have the key to a lot of the hardest-looking words there are. (Consider **a-poc'-ry-phal,** meaning "of doubt-ful authorship or authority.")

gh is another dragon to slay. Unlike **ph,** you can't always count on it. When it is silent, it often changes the sound of the vowel or vowel digraphs before it. That is, **light** spelled without the gh would be **lit,** and **ought** without it would be **out. Caught** seems to be an exception; without the gh it would still be **caught.** In a few other words, the g is pro-nounced and the h is silent.

For the Teacher

A small child will find this page too difficult. He might be helped to read only the one or two easiest words in each section. Or read them for him one at a time and have him repeat them after you.

Even a more advanced pupil cannot be expected to guess the pronounciation of these words if they are new to him. **ough** has six different pronunciations ($\bar{o}$, *awf, ŭf, ou, aw, $\overline{oo}$*). Read the words to him and have him read them after you. Tell him this page is a collection of the worst demons in the language. After this everything else is easy. For some reason the poor reader does not seem to be particularly troubled by the different sounds of **ough** but he does confuse **bought** and **brought,** for which there seems no excuse.

Words ending in le (əl)

page 242

To the Student

Now we come to words which have syllables ending in **le.** You remember that **le** is pronounced *əl.* Notice that when there are two consonants before the **le** there is a short vowel sound in the first syllable. If there is a single consonant be-fore **le,** the vowel will be long. If there are two vowels in the first syllable, the sound will be long anyway, as in **steeple.**

For the Teacher

Now is a good time to introduce the idea of the syllable, since we are starting on polysyllabic words. After the learner reads the **le** words, show him that they have two syllables by pronouncing them with a decided pause between syllables. Then say the following words and let him repeat them and count the syllables on his fingers as he does so:

box	berry	afterwards	transportation
automobile		establishment	disorganization

All remedial students will tell you that they do not understand about syllables; show them that they speak in syllables whether they know it or not.

For the beginner one column of **le** words will be enough.

sh is spelled five ways
page 243

To the Student

On this page we see that the *sh* sound is written in five ways. *sh* in the middle of long words is generally spelled **ti, si,** or **ci. Partition** has **ti** pronounced two different ways.

ch has three sounds
page 244

To the Student

ch is pronounced in three ways. In words from the Anglo-Saxon, it has the *ch* sound; in Greek words the *k* sound; and it is *sh* in words of French origin. Also we hear the *ch* sound in words that are not spelled with **ch** but with **tu,** as in **future,** etc.

For the Teacher

Chrysalis and **chrysanthemum** are put in for fun. Your student can read them if he proceeds calmly. Tell him that **chrys** is a Greek root meaning "golden." A **chrysanthemum** is a golden flower. A **chrysalis** is a golden sheath. Have him read **chrysanthemum** three times by syllables and then see if he can write it from memory, as he says the syllables. Since none of his friends and few of his relatives can spell it, it will do a lot for his ego!

zh

page 245

To the Student

The *zh* sound has no rightful spelling of its own at all, and is written with an *s* or a *z*. If you are spelling a word with this sound, remember it is never spelled with **ss**. **Occasion** could not be spelled with two s's.

A SPELLING RULE

page 246

For the Teacher

Point with your pencil as you read the words. Make up brief sentences for each word, as "A **diner** is one who dines," and "Eat your **dinner**."

Say, "If you want to turn **pine** into **pining**, you drop the **e** and add **ing**. The i still has its long sound, **pine, pining,** and we also have **pined,** ending in **d.**

"Now if you start with **pin,** which has the short sound of i (ĭ) and you want to turn it into **pinning,** you can't just add **ing** or you come up with **pining**, with the long sound of **i** (*ī*) again. So we put in another **n** and get **pinning**. This second **n** makes the first **i** keep its short sound. Also we need two **n**'s to keep the short sound in **pinned**."

The same thing is true with **hope** and **hop**, **dine** and **din**. Repeat the explanation and have the student read the words.

Teach the rules. The spelling rule is taught in school and means nothing to the child who doesn't know his long and short vowel sounds.

HOMONYMS
page 247

To the Student

Homonyms are words that sound alike but are spelled differently and have different meanings. Here are a few of the common ones. Now you can see why it is an advantage to have more than one way to spell a sound. You can tell the meaning from the spelling.

REGULAR IRREGULARITIES
page 248

For the Teacher

This page contains eight phonograms that will clear up a lot of difficult words. These "regular irregularities" occur very frequently. Our spelling follows a more regular pattern than most people realize. **er** pronounced **air** occurs only in accented syllables.

Again, only the simpler words need be read by a beginner.

To the Student

The endings of the words at the bottom of the page look as though they should have long vowel sounds, but instead they have short ones.

COMMON WORDS WITH QUEER SPELLINGS

page 250

To the Student

Here are some of the very common words that don't seem to be spelled as they ought to be. The first ten have a silent **e** on the end and still have short vowel sounds. These you will just have to learn to read and spell. If you try to figure out what is irregular about them and how the vowels are sounded (**o** says ŭ) and what the silent consonants are, it will help you to remember them. You just have to accept the fact that these words are spelled queerly.

LONG WORDS

page 252

To the Student

By now you should be able to read almost any word that is in your speaking vocabulary. Here are some long ones which are divided into syllables and then printed as whole words. When you meet long words like these, you will have no trouble with them if you just start at the beginning and work through the word. You will find they are all made up of syllables that you recognize. No one can take in a long word like **transportation** the first time he meets it in one swoop. Instead, read it by syllables, think what it means, read it once more, and after that you will recognize it at a glance.

For the Teacher

The student has been trained in the previous pages to read every one of these syllables. He should not have to guess at the pronunciation or to sound them out letter by letter.

Explain to the student that when he meets a new word he may have to try more than one vowel sound or more than one sound for **ch.** If he comes out with a pronunciation that is almost right but not quite, the right pronunciation will probably come to mind at once. For instance, if he read **hospital** with the ō sound, the right pronunciation would be easy to guess.

UNFAMILIAR WORDS

page 254

To the Student

Now you can read all the words in your speaking vocabulary. When you come to a word you have never heard before you can read it except that you may not be sure where the accent is placed, and then you have to consult a dictionary.

Here is a page of words that may not be familiar to you. They are written below, divided into syllables with the accents marked. There is one important thing to remember— that the long words in English normally come from the Latin. Their spelling is perfectly regular, and they are made up of the same old syllables over and over again, so they are really very easy to read. Just for fun, we have put down the two longest words in the language. If you can read them, you should be awarded a diploma right here and now.

For the Teacher

These words are deliberately chosen as difficult ones that the student probably would not understand. After he looks at the first six words, show him these same words divided into syllables. Show him how different these words sound if you put the accent on some other syllable. Try saying **at mos' phere**, with the accent on the second syllable; it sounds quite different from **atmosphere**.

To the Student

In reading you will meet words whose meaning you do not know. If you take the trouble to pronounce every new word you meet, you will build up your vocabulary rapidly.

People who have done a great deal of reading have learned the meaning of thousands of words simply by guessing the meaning over and over again from the context, without ever consulting a dictionary. If you come across some word, like **truculent**, several times and still can't figure out what it means, you will finally be driven by sheer curiosity to look it up. Educated people, however, make a friend of the dictionary and consult it much more often than the uneducated. An accurate vocabulary is the mark of an educated person.

A LAST NOTE TO THE TEACHER

This is as far in the system as many children will need to go. Have your student spend half an hour reading long words in the dictionary to convince him that he is capable of anything, then find the right book and let him read aloud.

Spelling

This book may be used as a speller. Go back as far as necessary, have the student read selected words, then write them while he says the syllables, not the letters. Later you dictate them to him. He should be able to teach himself the spelling of a new word by reading it once or twice. In spelling he starts with the sounds of the spoken word and represents them with letters, which is the opposite of the reading process. A person who reads with complete comprehension of phonics learns to spell hundreds of words without practice.

A list of the spelling demons that require extra work is included at the end of the text. If you want your child to be a really good speller, have him write a little bit every day. Tell him the words he asks for and have him keep an alphabetical list. He should have the spelling demons handy to refer to like a dictionary.

Through the Phonic Barrier

THE CONSONANTS

The **c, g,** and **s** have two sounds; qu = *kw;* x = *ks*

b c d f g h j k l m n
   c   **g**

p qu r s t v w x y z
       s

RULE 1

c says *s* before **e i y**

cent city mice cycle

c says *k* before **a o u**

cat cow cut

g says *g* before **a o u**

game go gum

ge says *j* at the end of a word

age bridge

THE VOWELS

The long vowels say their names

a	e	i	o	u	y
ā	ē	ī	ō	ū	ī

Fat Ed is not up

The short vowels are sounded as in "Fat Ed is not up."

a	e	i	o	u	y
ă	ĕ	ĭ	ŏ	ŭ	ĭ

a also says **ah** (ȧ)

SPECIAL VOWEL SOUNDS

oo
ŏŏ

oo
ōō

ou
ow
ou

oy
oi
oy

aw
au
aw

Read:

oo	ou	oy	aw
oo	ow	oi	au

SPECIAL CONSONANT SOUNDS

th
th

ch
ch

-ng
ng

sh
sh

wh
hw

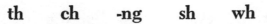

Read:

th   ch   -ng   sh   wh

VOWEL DIGRAPHS

These generally say the long sound of the first letter:

ā	ē	ī	ō	ū
ai	ee	ie	oa	ue
ay	ea		oe	ui
			ow	

Also:
ei and ey say ā or ē
ie says ī or ē
ew and eu say ū or ōō

VOWELS FOLLOWED BY R

er   ir   ur

or   ar

Examples: her   fir   fur   or   car

RULE 2

One vowel followed by one or two consonants is short.
Add an **e**, and the vowel becomes long. The final **e** is silent.

at	et	it	ot	ut
ate	ete	ite	ote	ute

CONSONANT BLENDS

br	sp	bl	sk
cr	spr	cl	sm
fr	st	fl	sn
dr	str	gl	sw
gr	sc	sl	squ
pr	sc	pl	tw
tr	scr	spl	
thr			
shr			

Also:

chr (*kr*)
sch (*sk*)

ODD WAYS OF WRITING
SOME CONSONANT SOUNDS

Silent first letters

wr (*r*)   gn (*n*)

kn (*n*)   ps (*s*)

Other oddities

ph (*f*)

gh (*f, g,* or silent)

rh (*r*)

gu (*g*)

ti

si ⎫ say (*sh*)

ci

le says (ə*l*)

ble	kle
cle	ple
dle	sle
fle	tle
gle	zle

At this point you have learned all the "bricks" with which printed words are built.

COMBINING A CONSONANT WITH
LONG AND SHORT VOWELS

ra wa ta ya pa sa da fa ga ha

ja ka la za ca va ba na ma

we re te ye pe se de fe ge he

je ke le ze ce ve be ne me

wi ri ti pi si di fi gi hi ji

ki li zi ci vi bi ni mi

ro to po so do fo go ho jo ko

lo zo vo bo no mo yo co

ru tu yu pu su du fu gu hu ju

ku lu zu cu vu bu nu mu

COMBINING A CONSONANT BLEND WITH LONG AND SHORT VOWELS

tra dra cra spra pra

cha gla pla sta

tre dre cre spre pre

che gle ple ste

tri dri cri spri pri

chi gli pli sti

tro dro cro spro pro

cho glo plo sto

tru dru cru spru pru

chu glu plu stu

A/a

at	ate	ack	ank
am	ame	act	ang
an	ane	aff	al
as	ase	aft	
ax		amp	(aw)
ap	ape	ant	al
ad	ade	ance	alt
af	afe	anch	all
.ag	age	adge	
ak	ake	atch	arc
al	ale	ath	ark
.ac	ace	ash	ard
ab	abe	asp	arl
av	ave	ast	arm
az	aze	ass	arn
(ar)	-are	and	art
		ānge	arb
		āste	arp
		āthe	arge

A words

cab	map	wade	cape
pad	scrap	made	tape
lad	has	blade	gape
sad	class	safe	drape
mad	mass	cage	shape
bag	glass	rage	scrape
rag	pass	badge	hate
pal	brass	cake	rate
ham	grass	lake	plate
ram	hat	make	crate
jam	sat	take	skate
man	chat	pale	slate
ran	rat	male	gate
pan	tax	sale	cave
fan	babe	same	brave
Jap	face	shame	knave
slap	lace	blame	gave
clap	space	pane	shave
flap	fade	lane	wave

blaze	spank	bath	harp
gaze	dance	path	large
case	glance	cash	charge
chase	chance	crash	all
phrase	pant	clasp	ball
bare	plant	past	wall
share	scant	last	salt
care	grant	hard	malt
rare	ranch	lard	sang
square	branch	park	rang
pack	range	lark	clang
lack	strange	snarl	sprang
tact	change	harm	gang
fact	haste	farm	and
chaff	paste	barn	hand
camp	bathe	yarn	land
damp	scratch	cart	stand
lamp	catch	chart	strand
tank	latch	garb	sand

E/e

eb	ebe	ebb	epth
· ec	ece	eck	ess
ed	ede	edge	esh
ef	efe	eft	est
· eg	ege	egg	eth
el	ele	ell	ext
em	eme	elf	
en	ene	emp	erb
ep	epe	end	erd
es	ese	ent	erk
et	ete	enth	erch
ev	eve	ench	
ex		ence	eng
ez	eze	ept	ength
ek	eke		
(er)	ere		

E WORDS

ebb	theme	self	hence
red	these	shelf	kept
Ned	eve	hemp	slept
fed	Pete	tempt	depth
fled	peck	bend	less
bed	neck	when	yes
sled	check	lend	chess
egg	edge	trend	mesh
leg	ledge	sent	guess
Meg	sledge	cent	flesh
gem	left	scent	west
hem	sell	went	best
ten	cell	bent	quest
pen	tell	lent	Beth
men	yell	wreck	her
yet	jell	tenth	herd
let	well	here	jerk
set	swell	bench	perch
next	quell	wrench	length
when	squelch	fence	strength

I/i

it	ite	ick	ist
ib	ibe	ich	ith
ic	ice	ict	itch
id	ide	idge	
if	ife	ift	ird
ig	ige	ilk	irl
ik	ike	ill	irm
il	ile	ilt	irt
im	ime		irp
in	ine	ince	irch
ip	ipe	inge	irst
is	ise	inch	irth
iv	ive	int	
ix		imp	īld
iz	ize	impse	īnd
(ir)	ire	ish	ind
		isk	
		isp	ink
		iss	ing

I WORDS

hit	lid	mile	side
bit	cliff	smile	life
flit	dig	file	strife
pit	bill	rise	ridge
sit	hill	wise	bridge
sip	pill	trim	Mike
skip	trill	hire	like
lip	fill	mire	hike
slip	bib	fire	hive
clip	rib	sire	live
chip	bin	wire	dive
drip	fin	dire	drive
trip	sin	bite	bribe
his	pin	white	mine
kiss	him	site	thine
hiss	Jim	quite	dine
miss	mice	snipe	fine
did	rice	ripe	line
hid	slice	hide	swine

scribe	with	limp	chirp
time	rich	glimpse	shirt
fringe	which	crisp	squirt
sick	prize	lisp	birch
quick	hitch	wisp	birth
Dick	pitch	fix	mirth
trick	ditch	six	wind
prick	dish	strict	wild
lint	wish	guise	child
hint	fish	guilt	mild
mint	mist	quilt	kind
sift	wrist	sir	find
lift	milk	stir	sing
drift	silk	dirt	ring
sink	since	flirt	fling
drink	mince	bird	swing
think	prince	first	spring
pinch	risk	third	thing
chintz	whisk	firm	bring

O/o

ob	obc	ock	orch
oc	oce	odge	ord
od	ode	omp	orge
of	ofe	ompt	ork
og	oge	ond	orm
ok	oke	osh	orn
ol	ole	ōld	ort
om	omc	ōlt	orth
on	one	ōst	
op	ope	otch	(*aw*)
os	ose		oft
ot	ote		oss
ov	ove	ong	ost
ox			
oz	oze		
(or)	ore		

O words

cob	not	stone	fore
knob	clot	hope	snore
sob	blot	rope	store
snob	plot	mope	core
pod	trot	slope	shore
God	fox	those	score
dog	box	chose	chore
hog	robe	nose	block
frog	probe	rose	stock
fog	rode	go	sock
doll	joke	lo	lock
Tom	poke	note	gosh
Don	hole	quote	pomp
hop	mole	wrote	prompt
mop	home	cove	pond
pop	dome	rove	fond
drop	Rome	strove	bond
stop	tone	froze	dodge
hot	zone	for	lodge

porch	form	notch	gong
torch	born	colt	strong
scorch	corn	bolt	wrong
Ford	torn	hold	soft
cord	short	bold	boss
forge	fort	told	toss
fork	sport	most	loss
cork	snort	post	lost
stork	north	song	cost
storm	Scotch	long	frost

U/u

ub	ube	uck	ush
uc	uce	uff	ust
ud	ude	uft	unce
uf	ufe	ulch	
ug	uge	ulge	
uk	uke	ulk	urb
ul	ule	* ull	urch
um	ume	* ull	urf
un	une	ulp	urge
up	upe	ulse	url
us	use	ump	urn
ut	ute	und	urst
uv	uve	unk	urt
ux		unt	urve
uz		unge	
(ur)	ure	unch	ung
		udge	
		uch	
		utch	

* As in pull and hull.

U words

hut	cub	trust	punch
but	pulse	junk	scrunch
shut	plunge	bunk	dupe
cup	rub	hunk	use
cut	run	hump	fuse
nut	spun	mule	rule
bud	fun	chunk	dude
mud	pun	drunk	surge
cuff	sun	skunk	curve
hug	bun	trunk	huge
bug	hum	sunk	gulch
rug	sum	cure	fume
mug	just	sure	duke
dug	must	pure	tube
dull	crust	cube	tune
gull	gust	cute	fund
pull	dust	crunch	hunt
full	rust	lunch	grunt
tub	thrust	bunch	tuck

luck	fudge	turn	burst
truck	bulge	burn	rush
suck	bulk	spurn	hush
duck	pulp	lurch	mush
chuck	June	church	blush
cluck	jump	puff	tuft
pluck	bump	much	sung
Duz	jug	such	rung
tux	purr	clutch	flung
dunce	blur	curb	swung
fund	slur	curl	lung
grudge	fur	surf	buzz
judge	cur	hurt	fuzz

Y/y

When **y** is a vowel, it is pronounced $\bar{\imath}$ or $\breve{\imath}$ or like the **y** in **party.**

$\bar{\imath}$	$\breve{\imath}$	
by	system	party
fly	nymph	newly
flying	gym	nicely
sky	cylinder	hardy
why	bicycle	happy
tying		hardly
dying		baby
		truly

WORDS WITH VOWEL DIGRAPHS

ay (ā)

day	may	play	tray	spray
say	bay	gray	stay	sway

ai (ā)

ait	ain	aim	ail	aise

oa (ō)

oat	oaf	oak	oal	oam
oan	oax	oach	oap	oast

ee (ē)

eet	eep	eese	eed	eef
eel	eech	eece	een	eem

Now read these words:

wait	boat	coax	sleet	feel
paint	loaf	coach	sleep	speech
pain	soak	coast	geese	fleece
claim	goal	boast	need	green
pail	loan	moan	beef	seen
raise	foam	groan	seek	seem

ea has three sounds

ea ($\bar{e}$)

beat	leap	tease	bead
beak	seal	beach	leave
leaf	bean	cream	yeast
read	dream	beast	cheat
ear	dear	tear	clear

ea ($\breve{e}$)

read	head	bread	health
dead	breath	lead	instead
wealth	tread	meadow	leather
threat	spread	dread	weather
meant	behead	thread	feather

ea ($\bar{a}$)

great	steak	break	wear
bear	tear	pear	

ear sometimes says **er**

earn	learn	heard	earl

oe (ō)

toe	hoe	goes	toes	foe

ow (ō)

low	bow	tow	show
snow	throw	grown	blow
thrown	bowl	blown	flown

ie (ī)

pie	tie	flies	tries
skies	cries	dried	cried
die	fries	died	fried

ie (ē)

chief	field	fiend	grief
brief	fierce	belief	achieve
niece	piece	yield	believe
pierce	relief	shield	shriek

igh (ī)

nigh	sigh	high	right
night	light	sight	slight
fright	might	flight	bright

Here the silent gh makes the i long and turns lit into light, fit into fight, sit into sight, and mit into might.

$$\left.\begin{array}{l} \text{ei} \\ \text{ey} \end{array}\right\} \text{say } \bar{e} \text{ or } \bar{a}$$

$$\bar{a}$$

eigh always says $\bar{a}$

eight	freight
weight	neighbor
thcy	their
obey	vein
convey	veil

$$\bar{e}$$

cei always says $s\bar{e}$

receive	ceiling
key	either
monkey	neither

SPECIAL VOWEL SOUNDS

ou

ow

cow	town
how	owl
now	frown
bow	growl
plow	prowl
row	howl
down	crowd

ou

out	mouse
our	mouth
shout	round
ground	flour
house	loud
hour	cloud
spout	pound
sound	south

aw

aw

paw	drawn
saw	shawl
raw	crawl
claw	lawn

au

haul
fault
cause
pause

oy

oi

oil	point
boil	joint
soil	void
join	voice
coin	noise

oy

boy
boys
toy
joy
oyster

ōō and ū

oo		ew
room	too	chew
stool	do	shrewd
school	to	knew
food	poor	grew
toot	moor	brew

ue	ui
true	fruit
clue	suit
due	pursuit
glue	recruit
Tuesday	

ŏŏ

oo		u
look	hood	put
took	wood	pull
book	foot	full

ODD WAYS OF WRITING
SOME CONSONANT SOUNDS

Three curiosities with silent first letters

kn	wr		gn	
know	write	wretch	gnaw	sign
knew	wrote	wrong	gnat	align
knee	wrap	wry	gnome	reign
knife	wreath	wrench	gnash	feign

Four more curiosities

rh (r)	gu (g)
rhythm	guard
rhyme	guild
rhetoric	guilt
myrrh	guess
rhinoceros	guest
rhubarb	guarantee

ph (f)

phone	phonics	phrase
graph	phonograph	photograph
telegraph	Philippines	Philadelphia

gh

gh says *f* in:

tough	rough	enough
cough	trough	laugh

gh says *g* in:

ghastly	ghost	aghast

gh is silent in:

caught	ought	thought
though	light	through
eight	sleigh	straight
dough	bought	thorough
night	brought	neighbor

Words ending in le (əl)

ble	able	table	rabble
cle	circle	uncle	bicycle
dle	paddle	ladle	handle
fle	rifle	trifle	scuffle
gle	gargle	wiggle	struggle
kle	tackle	twinkle	sparkle
ple	apple	maple	steeple
tle	little	battle	turtle
zle	puzzle	sizzle	dazzle

The sound *sh* is spelled five ways

sh		she		shoot
ti	-tion	nation		station
		education		starvation
		attention		partition
		vacation		vaccination
		transportation		
	-tial	initial	spatial	partial
	-tious	cautious		captious
si	-sion	mission	pension	session
ci	-cial	special	facial	
	-cious	precious	gracious	spacious
	-cient	sufficient	deficient	
ch		machine	Chicago	

ch has three sounds

ch (*ch*)   **church**   **child**

ch (*sh*)   **machine**   **Chicago**

ch (*k*)   **school**   **scheme**

                ache   **stomach**

                chrome   **chronic**

                Christmas   **chrysalis**

                Christian   **chrysanthemum**

The sound *ch* is spelled two ways

ch	church	chicken
tu	nature	actual
	future	

zh

There is one more sound which you hear in the following words. We write the sound *zh*, but it is spelled s or z, never ss.

treasure	occasion	seizure
pleasure	collision	azure
leisure	casual	

A SPELLING RULE

pine	pin	hope	hop
pining	(pining)	hoping	(hoping)
	pinning		hopping
pined	pinned	hoped	hopped
dine	din	swim	hug
dining	dinning	swimmer	hugged
dined	dinned	swimming	hugging
diner	dinner		

Spelling

1. When a word ends in **e** drop the **e** before adding **ing**, **er**, or **ed**.

2. Before adding **ing**, **ed**, or **er** to a one-syllable word with a short vowel, double the last consonant to keep the vowel short.

Reading

With words ending in **ing**, **er** and **ed**, the first vowel is long before one consonant and short before two consonants.

HOMONYMS

their	there	one	won
no	know	blue	blew
wait	weight	whole	hole
heel	heal	write	right
new	knew	sight	site

to	too	two
vane	vein	vain

REGULAR IRREGULARITIES

wor generally says wer

word	worst	worship
work	worth	worms
world	worry	

er says air in some words

there	herring	Bering Strait
where	periscope	perish
ferry	ceremony	very

ir says ear in some words

irrelevant	irritate	irradiate

Unaccented suffixes have short vowel sounds

ain

captain   Britain   certain   fountain

age

baggage   manage   advantage   damage

ive

active   effective   detective   defective

ous

famous   marvelous   dangerous   mountainous

ine

examine   imagine   engine   discipline

COMMON WORDS WITH
QUEER SPELLINGS

1. Short vowels instead of long (o says ŭ)

some	live	again
come	give	been
love	were	does
glove	are	said
have	done	

2. Different vowel sounds than you would expect

many	four	do	move
any	you	to	prove
what	your	into	pretty
carry	marry		

3. Find the silent consonants

isle	comb	doubt	answer
island	lamb	debt	yacht
salmon	climb	often	hour
whistle	bomb	palm	two
limb	calm	psalm	

4. Just queer

one	woman	could	walk
once	women	would	talk
eye	of	should	chalk

LONG WORDS

kang a roo	kangaroo
hel i cop ter	helicopter
car pen ter	carpenter
air plane	airplane
sa tel lite	satellite
tel e scope	telescope
par a chute	parachute
pro pel ler	propeller
tri an gle	triangle
sub ma rine	submarine
com mo tion	commotion
ed u ca tion	education
trans por ta tion	transportation
trans par ent	transparent

trans for ma tion	transformation
con ver sa tion	conversation
as ton ish ment	astonishment
pun ish ment	punishment
pave ment	pavement
pay ment	payment
ev i dence	evidence
con tain er	container
re tain er	retainer
con cen tra ting	concentrating
hap haz ard	haphazard
buz zard	buzzard
med i cine	medicine

UNFAMILIAR WORDS

analysis	atmosphere
composition	equivalent
esoteric	calumniate

antitransubstantiation

antidisestablishmentarianism

a nal' y sis	at' mos phere
com' po si' tion	e quiv' a lent
es' o ter' ic	ca lum' ni ate

an ti tran' sub stan' ti a' tion

an ti dis' es tab' lish men ta' ri an ism

anti dis establish men ta ri an ism

SUPPLEMENTARY WORK

This work has been found valuable for the high-school or college student who has been reading inaccurately for years. It will focus his attention on things that have been confusing him and will clear up many problems. The misspellings on page 269 provide valuable drill in accurate reading because it is not possible to guess the pronunciation. Except for the French words, this sort of thing is not necessary for a young child or for one who was started correctly in reading.

WORDS OF FRENCH ORIGIN

English words of French origin offer special difficulty because they are based on French, instead of English, phonics.

eau says $\bar{o}$
>   beau   château   tableau   trousseau
>   (In **beauty** and **beautiful** we have
>   anglicized the pronunciation)

The letter **i** says $\bar{e}$; **que** says k
  technique   antique   physique   clique   pique

gue says g; **ngue** says ng
>   fatigue   intrigue   tongue   harangue

The final consonant is silent, and **et** is pronounced $\bar{a}$
  bouquet   croquet   ballet   sachet

ch says sh or k, never ch
 chamois   chauffeur   machine   Charlotte   technique

é and **ée** say $\bar{a}$
>   fiancée   risqué   negligée   protégé

ge is pronounced zh
>   loge   garage   barrage

ou says $\bar{oo}$, $\breve{oo}$ or $\bar{o}$, never ou
>   boudoir   silhouette   bouquet

IRREGULAR VOWEL DIGRAPHS

Some vowel digraphs like **oa** and **ee** are perfectly regular. Others are not. We have made up a rule which accounts for many nonphonetic words.

The rule is that vowel digraphs are pronounced: (1) usually like the long sound of the first letter; (2) sometimes like the long sound of the second letter; (3) less frequently like the short sound of the second letter; (4) and least frequently like the short sound of the first letter. Some examples are missing, we admit. Can you supply them? There are some other pronunciations, too.

Many of these words are spelling "demons." If you concentrate on the sound of the digraph as you read them, you will have no trouble learning to spell them.

	ui		**ai**		**ay**
$\bar{u}$	suit	$\bar{a}$	wait	$\bar{a}$	say
$\bar{\imath}$	guide	$\bar{\imath}$	aisle	$\bar{\imath}$	ay
$\breve{\imath}$	build	$\breve{\imath}$	captain	$\breve{\imath}$	always
$\breve{u}$	——	$\breve{a}$	plaid	$\breve{a}$	——
$\bar{oo}$	bruise				

ie		ey		ei	
ī	pie	ĭ	money	ē	receive
ē	chief	ē	key	ī	height
ĭ	mischief	ī	eye	ĭ	forfeit
ĕ	friend	ā	obey	ā	eight
		ĕ	——	ĕ	heifer

What are the vowel sounds in these spelling demons?

	ei	ie
weird	perceive	sieve
seize	heir	siege
leisure	seismograph	kerchief
obeisance	kaleidoscope	tries
sleight	surfeit	replies
reign	foreign	fierce

The vowel combinations **oi** and **oy** are regular, but **au,** **ow,** and **ou** are not. The joker of the lot is **ou,** which has at least eight pronunciations. Do not try to learn these eight; just learn to spell these particular words.

	au			**ou**			
au	taught	*ou*	out	$\bar{oo}$	soup
ă	aunt	*ō*	soul	$\breve{oo}$	should
ā	gauge	*ū*	Houston	*er*	glamour
		ŭ	double	*aw*	bought

What sounds do *ou* and *au* have in these words?

group	famous
croup	laugh
cantaloup	laughter
country	restaurant
courteous	exhausted
journey	jaunt

HELP IN ELIMINATING REVERSALS IN SPELLING AND READING

Section 1

On the lefthand side of this page, we have some of the same old digraphs or diphthongs which have a single sound within a syllable. On the righthand side, the same letters happen to occur in reverse order, but always they are read as two separate vowel sounds, each in a different syllable. The word is divided into syllables between these vowels.

ai	train	i·a	dial, Columbia, trial, Siam,
	Britain		diary, diaphanous, piano
au	fraud	u·a	truant, spiritual
	inexhaustible		
oe	toe	*e·o	stereotype, cameo, beauteous
ou	out	u·o	duo, virtuous
	sprouting		
oa	boat	a·o	chaotic
	unloading		

* *There is positively no excuse for the word "people"!*

Section 2

In the first two columns we have pairs of digraphs which are reversals of each other and in the last, words which have these same two letters side by side, but where again the words are divided into syllables between the two vowels. **ae** is a new digraph occurring only in a few Greek words. It says *ē*.

ie	pie	ei	seize	i·e	client, orient,
	believe		weird		variety, science,
			inveigh	e·i	reinforce, deity
ui	fruit			u·i	ruin
	unsuitable			i·u	diurnal, triumphant
eu	feud	ue	cue	e·u	deum
	deuce		accrued	u·e	duet, cruet, fluent
	Teutonic				
ea	bead	ae	Aesop	e·a	cereal, beatitude,
	repeated		Thermopylae		create, Aegean Sea
			Aegean Sea		
oi	point			o·i	heroic
	embroider			i·o	inferior, pious,
					glorious

Section 3

Obviously you can have vowels before and after the letter **r**. The first column has the regular vowel-**r** combinations you have learned, with examples. The second column contains words in which the vowel follows the **r**. The **r** is then just the first letter of a syllable followed by a vowel, or is part of a beginning blend. In the third column, words are divided into syllables between the vowel and the **r**. There will be no trouble reading or spelling these words if you sound them from left to right.

ur	burnt	**ru**	brunt	**uranium**
	Turk		truck	
	spurn		prunes	
	spurious		truculent	
er	stern	**re**	rest	**erase**
	fervent		frequent	**berate**
	perhaps		prevent	
ir	girl	**ri**	grill	**siren**
	irradiate		rival	
	satirical		intricate	
	affirm		infringe	
ar	star	**ra**	rats	**arise**
	sharper		shrapnel	**around**
	warp		wrap	

or	form	ro	from	prorate
	formidable		affront	
	restoring		astronomy	
	torment		introduce	

Section 4

In these words, we see **io, ia, ua,** which are not digraphs, occurring in a single syllable. Figure out why.

caution	precious	pension	initial	special
Russia	familiar	Guam		persuade

HOW DO YOU DIVIDE WORDS INTO SYLLABLES?

Written syllables do not correspond exactly with spoken ones. In writing, we divide after the vowel when it is long, as in **ra bies,** and after the consonant if the vowel is short, as in **cab i net.** In speaking, we always put the consonant with the following vowel and say **ca bi net, ra dish, cre dit.** So here we have a thoroughly arbitrary distinction between the way we pronounce a word and the way we divide the same word at the end of a line of print.

Study the words on pages 265 and 266. The first column has words with closed first syllables and double consonants. These are divided between the consonants.

The words in the second column start with open syllables ending in long vowel sounds. These are divided after the first vowel.

The words in the last column have a short first vowel, followed by a single consonant and so are always divided after the consonant.

This is not a complete rule for dividing into syllables, but it will help in many instances. Written words are divided according to their historical origins; you will often have to consult the dictionary to find the correct way to divide them. For instance, **vaccinate** and **accurate** both have syllables ending in vowels, in which the vowels are short. These syllables are unaccented.

In teaching yourself to spell these words, read them by syllables mentally dividing according to the dictionary practice, not according to the way you would ordinarily say them. Pronounce both of the double consonants in words in the first column. Thus you will get a picture of the word which will help solve the old spelling problem, "One consonant or two?"

Notice there must be two **cc**'s in words like **accident, succeed,** and **vaccinate** because there is both a *k* and an *s* sound.

THREE KINDS OF WORDS

1. A closed syllable ends in a consonant; the vowel is short.

Example: **rab** (*răb*)

2. An open syllable ends in a vowel which has the long sound.

Example: **ra** (*rā*)

closed syllable

rabble	rab′ ble
cabbage	cab′ bage
riddle	rid′ dle
adder	ad′ der
taffy	taf′ fy
raffle	raf′ fle
affable	af′ fa ble
accident	ac′ ci dent
succeed	suc ceed′
vaccinate	vac′ ci nate
accurate	ac′ cu rate
occasion	oc ca′ sion

open syllable		closed syllable	
rabies	ra′ bies	cabinet	cab′ i net
cable	ca′ ble	probably	prob′ a bly
ladle	la′ dle	radish	rad′ ish
radio	ra′ di o	credit	cred′ it
profess	pro fess′	preference	pref′ er ence
prefer	pre fer′	preface	pref′ ace
professor	pro fes′ sor	profit	prof′ it
recess	re cess′	facet	fac′ et
locate	lo′ cate	decorate	dec′ or ate
December	De cem′ ber	pacify	pac′ i fy
decency	de′ cen cy	decorous	dec′ o rous
grocer	gro′ cer	second	sec′ ond

THE TEST

These are groups of two and three words that were confused and misread by high-school and college students. You should read them all perfectly.

burnt	silver	flatter
brunt	sliver	falter
Turk	slit	remained
truck	silt	remnant
spurn	spilt	plot
prunes	split	pilot
fervent	plaster	angle
frequent	psalter	angel
perhaps	thorn	sown
prevent	throne	snow
girl	swallow	plane
grill	sallow	panel
star	grid	pallor
rats	gird	player
sharper	cold	shrike
shrapnel	clod	shirk
warp	private	shirt
wrap	pirate	skirt
form	flout	hospital
from	fault	hospitable

pleat
pelt

irreverent
irrelevant

formerly
formally

stilt
slit

stride
stirred

not
ton

blame
balm

smile
simile

sheep
sleep

quite
quiet

sucker
ruckus

glide
gild

glitter
guilder

swarm
warms

shoulder
soldier
solider
solder

guard
gradual

reveled
relived

blot
bolt

starlet
startle

diary
dairy

ingenuous
ingenious

diet
deity

diction
direction

stereotype
stereoscope

waive
naive

united
untied

lamp
palm

marital
martial

slave
salve

advantage
adventure

calvary
cavalry

character
charter

undetermined
undermined

scared
scarred
sacred

TYPICAL ERRORS IN SPELLING

These words were misspelled on one term paper by one Stanford University sophomore. Since he paid to have the paper typed and the spelling corrected, his professor never knew what he missed. Incidentally, the student failed the course.

Read exactly what the student wrote and then read what he thought he was writing. Notice that only two misspellings are phonetic.

What can you learn from this? Just that you should read the word that you have written and see whether it says what you thought it did. Of course this poor fellow does not know enough phonics to do that, but by this time you do. Many people never think of this simple way to check their spelling.

devolped   developed

succeful   successful

suspetable   susceptible

coloinzation   colonization

lake   lack

centralizion   centralization

sacifed   sacrificed

languge   language

religon   religion

Molems   Moslems

laughting   laughing

equiptment equipment

muscules muscles

stringe stringy

abominal abominable

apponites opponents

porportant proportioned

presistant persistent

aquaitances acquaintances

appeartly apparently

secession succession

tempeture temperature

wreasling wrestling

licked liked

ritch rich

freakles freckles

hungery hungry

persaude persuade

valubale valuable

lissoned listened

volient violent

desortion distortion

avable available

GHOSTS

Are you troubled by ghosts when you spell? Almost everybody is. This phonics system should have cleared up many of them, but you will have to conjure up your own particular ones and exorcise them.

For example, do you wonder if there should be a **z** in **surprise?** If you do it is because the ghost of **prize** is haunting you.

Does the spelling of **forty** bother you? If so, it is because the ghosts of **four** and **fourteen** are haunting you.

One woman said she had to look up both **angel** and **angle** every time she spelled them. How would you straighten her out?

What are your own particular ghosts?

All words ending in **ance** and **ence, ant** and **ent, able** and **ible, ary** and **ery** have ghosts. You cannot tell from the sound how to spell these words; you must learn them or look them up in the dictionary every time.

ance	ant
resistance	resistant
attendance	attendant
extravagance	extravagant

ence	ent
persistence	persistent
confidence	confident
independence	independent

able	ible
desirable	inexhaustible
available	convertible
comfortable	sensible

ary	ery
dictionary	cemetery
secretary	confectionery

THE SPELLING DEMONS

ache	color	getting
after	coming	girl
again	cough	grammar
all right	could	guess
although	countries	half
always	country	having
among	dear	hear
answer	doctor	heard
any	does	helped
around	done	here
been	don't	hoarse
beginning	early	horse
believe	easy	hour
a blue dress	enough	house
break a leg	even	knew
built	every	know
business	February	laid
busy	finally	large
buy	first	largest
by	forty	like
can't	four	liked
captain	friend	loose
choose	get	lose

make	separate	trouble
making	shoes	truly
many	should	Tuesday
meant	since	used
minute	some	was
much	straight	wear
none	sugar	Wednesday
often	sure	week
one	tear the paper	were
once upon a time	their house	when
only	there they are	where
other	these	whether
people	they	which
piece of pie	things	while
raise	think	with
read	this	woman
ready	though	women
receive	through	won't
said	tired	would
say	too big	write
says	two cats	writing
seems	took	written
seen	tonight	wrote

Index